Zen Letters

Teachings of Yuanwu

Translated and edited by

J. C. Cleary and

Thomas Cleary

Shambhala
Boston & London
1994

Shambhala Publications, Inc.
Horticultural Hall
300 Massachusetts Avenue
Boston, Massachusetts 02115

9 8 7 6 5 4 3 2 1

First Edition
Printed in the United States of America on acid-free paper ♾
Distributed in the United States by Random House, Inc., and in Canada by Random House of Canada Ltd.

Library of Congress Cataloging-in-Publication Data

Yüan-wu, 1063–1135.
Zen letters: teachings of Yuanwu/translated and edited by J. C. Cleary and Thomas Cleary—1st ed.
p. cm.—
Translated from Chinese.
ISBN 0-87773-931-5 (acid-free paper)
1. Yüan-wu, 1063–1135—Correspondence. 2. Priests, Zen—China—Correspondence. 3. Zen Buddhism—Doctrines. I. Cleary, J. C. (Jonathan Christopher). II. Title. III. Series.
BQ998.U33A4 1994 93-21937
294.3′927—dc20 CIP

Zen Letters

Translators' Introduction

These letters were written by the Zen teacher known as Yuanwu to various friends, disciples, and associates—to women as well as to men, to people with families and worldly careers as well as to monks and nuns, to advanced adepts as well as to beginning seekers.

Yuanwu is best known as the author of the single most famous Zen book, *The Blue Cliff Record,* a collection of meditation cases with prose and verse comments. *The Blue Cliff Record* is an intricate web of Zen lore with endless subtleties. Here in these letters, Yuanwu delivers the Zen message in a more accessible form, in direct person-to-person lessons.

Yuanwu was a public spokesman for a tradition of wisdom that he saw coming down from time immemorial. In Yuanwu's Zen tradition, the man usually considered the historic founder of Buddhism was seen as just one buddha in a long line of enlightened ones extending back before history as we know it. In fact, Mahayana Buddhist texts regularly speak of "all the buddhas of the past, present, and future." Mahayana sutras like *The Flower Ornament Scripture* depict a vast universal process of enlightening teaching taking place in all worlds in all times through an infinite variety of forms.

The enlightened ones appeared in the world as teachers to alert people to the unsuspected fact that all of us possess an inherent potential for objective wisdom and unselfish compassion called buddha nature. These teachers meant to enable us to become aware of our buddha nature and to gain the use of it in our everyday life. Zen Buddhism, like all other branches of Mahayana Buddhism, maintains that it is the true destiny of every person to become enlightened.

From the perspective of Zen Buddhism, emotional allegiances, dogma, mechanical ritual, clerical careerism, and sectarian institutions must be seen as the enemies of true religion. True religion is by nature multiform; it consists of whatever practices and techniques and perspectives are effective in awakening the people of particular times and places and restoring their awareness of reality-in-itself, an absolute reality that contains all relative realities, without their getting trapped in any of their limited perspectives. No particular technique is worshipped as a panacea; all techniques are no more than expedient means employed by expert teachers to meet the specific needs of specific seekers.

The practice of Zen consists of a collection of liberative techniques that rest on a profound analysis of human perception and conditioning. In common with the seers of the other equivalent traditions around the world, the Zen adepts observed that ordinarily people are encased in a shell of emotion-laden conditioned perceptions that shape their motivations and limit their experience to a narrow range of standardized perspectives. Ordinarily people reify the concepts they have been unwittingly conditioned to believe in and to project upon the world—they see them as objectively true realities "out there," rather than as the arbitrary cultural constructs they are. Thus the Zen teachers actively worked to "untie the bonds and melt the sticking points" that were keeping their students' minds tied to habitual routines and conventional perceptions.

The Zen tradition, like all of Mahayana Buddhism, is invincibly optimistic about human possibilities—our true identity, our inherent buddha nature, can never be destroyed. It is our basic essence, and it is with us always, waiting to be activated and brought to life. "The sword that kills is the sword that brings life," runs an old Zen saying. The sword of wisdom that cuts away the conditioning and contrived activities that make up our false personality is what frees us and brings our enlightened potential out into the open.

The Mahayana seers did not agree with the modern materialists that we are basically animals forced by the demands of civilization to pit our feeble rationality and precarious moral sense against our submerged yet implacable instinctual drives. Nor did the Mahayana teachers follow the dualistic religions in seeing earthly life as an arena of sin and temptation where humankind is tested to qualify for a heavenly afterlife.

From the Mahayana point of view, once the human mind is washed clean of its conditioning and stripped of its delusions, the ordinary world is the site of enlightenment, suffused with the light of the Source, where liberated humans can wander at play, naked and free, living the life of wisdom and compassion.

Needless to say, Yuanwu (who was born in 1063 and died in 1135 CE) lived in a world in many ways very different from our own. In Yuanwu's time, Manhattan Island was a leafy forest crisscrossed with streams of clear water. The great cities of Mexico and Peru had not fallen to conquerors from across the sea. The Americas, Africa, Australia, and Oceania were home to a mosaic of diverse cultures, each a symbolic world unto itself, with its own rich history and tradition and way of life.

The Old World of Eurasia and North Africa had already seen empires come and go for millennia: armies, taxes, bureaucracies, castes of nobles and warriors vying for power, ancient traditions of scholarship and learning, populations of peasants and herders eking out a living. The West European onslaught against the rest of the world had not yet begun, and the world was home to immeasurably greater cultural diversity than it is today. No one had yet dared to assert that military superiority was the same thing as cultural superiority.

China in Yuanwu's time was dotted with giant urban centers that were the focal points of administration, commerce, and high culture. A network of officially recognized Buddhist institutions existed throughout the country. The ancient political philosophy of Confucianism had been revived and reworked under Buddhist influences. Taoism, too, was taking on new forms strikingly parallel to Zen. Chinese art and literature in the Song dynasty reached an unprecedented level of clarity and elegance.

But there were severe problems as well. Sporadic peasant uprisings broke out to challenge the growing inequality of wealth. A reform-minded faction in the imperial bureaucracy aroused the bitter opposition of the bulk of the landlord elite and went down to defeat. Though adequate to the task of keeping the peasantry in check, the bloated military establishment was about to go down to crushing defeat at the hands of a relative handful of barbarian invaders. Whatever its glories, the world of Song dynasty China was anything but the serene homeland of "the wisdom of the East" that some modern Westerners like to imagine.

Given the vast historical distance that separates us today from Song dynasty China, it is all the more remarkable how directly Yuanwu's letters communicate with us about the universal issues of the life of wisdom.

Maybe we mistakenly overestimate the differences between ourselves and the people of other times and places. The differences in the technological environments are obvious. But then, as now, people were caught up in their conditioning, driven on by their hopes and fears, eager to live up to socially defined goals and pursue images of the good life. Aren't the perceptions of most of us today still structured in terms of self and others, gain and loss, love and hate, desire and aversion? Don't we automatically assume that these dualities reflect an objective reality that leaves us no choice in the matter?

If so, then the message of Yuanwu's writings still holds something of great value for us. That message is multidimensional and unfolds more fully in the translation below. But for now, just a taste of the timeless wisdom:

> If you can cut off outward clinging to objects and inwardly forget your false ideas of self, things themselves are the true self, and the true self itself is things: things and true self are One Suchness, opening through to infinity.
>
> If you are attached to perception, then this is a perception—it is not the arriving at the Truth. Those who arrive at Truth transcend perception, but they manage to use perception without dwelling in perception. When you pass directly through perception and get free of it, it is all the fundamental Truth.

Zen Letters

"If where you stand is reality, then your actions have power"

Ever since antiquity, with excellence beyond measure, the saints and sages have experienced this Great Cause alone, as if planting great potential and capacity. By the power of their vows of compassion, they have brought forth direct indications of the One Thing that is most profound and most recondite, the common essence of all the myriad forms of being.

Without setting up stages, they abruptly transcend to realize this essence alone. Since before the time when nothing existed, this essence has been ever still and unmoved, determining the basis of all conscious beings. It permeates all times and is beyond all thought. It is beyond holy and ordinary and transcends all knowledge and views. It has never fluctuated or wavered: it is there, pure and naked and full of life. All beings, both animate and inanimate, have it complete within them.

That is why when Shakyamuni Buddha was first born, he immediately pointed to the heavens and to the earth and with a great lion's roar brought it right out in front. Then after he had left home and sought enlightenment for six years, he awakened at the sight of the morning star. In the end, on Vulture Peak, he initiated the Zen transmission by holding up a flower. All that was important is that we should possess the comprehension of this True Eye.

From the time of Shakyamuni, the True Eye was secretly transmitted through the twenty-eight Indian Patriarchs and the six Chinese Patriarchs. Those who did not know of the existence of the True Eye of enlightened perception thought that there was some kind of supernatural power or magical ability involved, and just spoke of going along with the waves and pursuing the current, never searching out the root of the transmission. If you discover its ultimate import, there is no need to poke into it.

In olden times, when Marquis Li met Zen master Shimen, Shimen said to him: "This is the business of a truly great man, not something that can be done by mere generals and high officials." Li understood right away, and expressed himself in verse:

To study the Way you must be an iron man
Lay hold of the mind and act decisively
Heading directly for unexcelled enlightenment
Paying no attention to any affirmation or denial

In general, when superior wisdom, excellent capacity, and natural potential are already there, it is just a matter of working to penetrate through surely and truly. When you put it to use, you command Great Potential and unfurl Great Function, moving even before any impulse to action, operating free of things.

Yantou said: "Spurning things is superior, following things is inferior. If we talk about battle, each one's strength is in the turning point."

If you can turn fast on top of things, then everything will submit to you, and everything will be in your grasp. Capturing and releasing, rolling up and rolling out—all can be transformed. At all times you remain peaceful and tranquil, without having anything whatsoever hanging on your mind. In action you accord with the situation and its potential, holding the means of discernment within yourself. Shifting and changing

and successfully adapting, you attain Great Freedom—all things and all circumstances open up before your blade, like bamboo splitting, all "bending down with the wind."

Therefore, if where you stand is reality, then your actions have power. Needless to say, leading brave heroes, commanding fierce warriors, routing powerful bandits, comforting the farmers, pacifying the nation, and assisting the work of restoring social harmony and cultural florescence all depend on this one revelation.

Turning the topmost key, achieving something that cannot be taken away in ten thousand generations, you see and hear the same as the ancient buddhas and share the same knowledge and functioning.

The Fourth Patriarch said: "If not for mind, there's no question of buddha."

Deshan said: "A buddha is just someone with no concerns."

Yongjia said: "It is not apart from *here,* always profoundly clear and still. If you search for it, you know you cannot see it."

Linji said: "The real being, with no status, is always going in and out through the doors of your face."

This is the substance of all these sayings.

Real Teaching and Real Learning

Since high antiquity, the source vehicle has been transcendence and direct realization, with teachers and apprentices joined in understanding, with nothing haphazard about it.

This is why the man who was to become the Second Zen Patriarch stood in the snow and cut off his arm to prove his sincerity to Bodhidharma, the First Patriarch. This is why the Sixth Patriarch worked pounding rice in the Fifth Patriarch's community at Huangmei. This is why other Zen adepts worked diligently for twenty or thirty years. How could the seal of approval be given lightly?

In general, genuine Zen teachers set forth their teachings only after observing the learners' situation and potential. Real teachers smelt and refine their students hundreds and thousands of times. Whenever the learner has any biased attachments or feelings of doubt, the teacher resolves them and breaks through them and causes the learner to penetrate through to the depths and let go of everything, so that the learner can realize equanimity and peace while in action. Real teachers transform learners so that they reach the stage where one cannot be broken, like a leather bag that can withstand any impact.

Only after this does the Zen teacher let the transformed student go forth to deal with people and help them. This is no small matter. If the student is incomplete in any respect, then the model is not right, and the unripe student comes out all uneven and full of excesses and deficiencies, and appears ridiculous to real adepts.

Therefore, in order to teach the Dharma, the ancient worthies worked for completeness and correctness, and clarity in all facets. This means inwardly having one's own practice as pure as ice and jade, and outwardly having a complete and well-rounded mastery of techniques, a perspicacious view of all conscious beings, and skill in interchange.

When such adepts met with potential learners, they examined each and every point in terms of the Fundamental. When the learners finally did understand, then the teachers employed techniques to polish and refine them. It was like transferring the water from one vessel into another vessel, with the utmost care not to spill a drop.

Among the methods the adepts employed, we see *driving off the plowman's ox* or *taking away the hungry man's food.* Unfathomable to spirits or ghosts, the genuine Zen adepts relied solely on the one great liberation. They didn't reveal the typical deformities of pretenders to enlightenment and "grow the horns characteristic of other species." At ease, without striving at contrived activity, they were true saints of discipline and virtue who had left behind the dusts of sensory attachments.

There is a saying by Bodhidharma: "Those whose actions and understanding were in accord we call *spiritual ancestors.*"

What Is a Zen Teacher?

Going on pilgrimages in search of enlightened teachers, going beyond convention—basically, this is done because of the importance of *the great matter of birth and death.*

Contacting people to help them is being a good spiritual

friend. Bringing to light the causal conditions of the great matter operates on the principle of mutual seeking and mutual aid.

Ever since ancient times, it is only those who are able to bear the responsibility of being a vessel of the Great Dharma who have been able to undertake the role of a Zen teacher and *stand like a wall a mile high.* These people have been tempered and refined in the blast furnace of the teachers of the Source, taking shape under the impact of their hammers and tongs, until they become real and true from beginning to end. Otherwise, they do not appear in the world as teachers. If they do appear, they are sure to startle the crowd and move the people. Because their own realization and acceptance of the responsibility of communicating Truth was not hasty and haphazard, when they passed it on to others they were not rushed or careless.

We all know the classic examples. Master Rang staying with the Sixth Patriarch at Caoqi for eight years. Mazu at Guanyin Temple. Deshan and Longtan. Yangshan and Guishan. Linji and Huangbo. In every case it took at least ten or twenty years of close association between teacher and pupil before the pupil was fully prepared to become a teacher himself.

That is why, with the genuine Zen teachers, every word and every phrase, every act and every state resonated with the music of gold and jade.

Virtually no one in the latter generations has been able to see into what they were doing. You will only be able to see where they were really at when you achieve transcendental realization and reach the stage that all the enlightened ones share in common.

I recall this story from olden times. Mazu asked Xitang, "Have you ever read the scriptural teachings?" Xitang said, "Are the scriptural teachings any different?" Mazu asked, "If you haven't read the scriptures, how will you be able to explain for people in various ways?" Xitang said, "I must care for my own sickness—how could I dare try to help other people?" Mazu said, "In your later years, you are sure to rise to greatness in the world." And that's the way it turned out later.

As we carefully consider the ancients, did they not achieve great penetration and great enlightenment toward the one great causal condition leading to transcendence? They cut off words and imagery and divorced themselves from the confusion of conditioned discrimination; they just knew for themselves, enjoying peace and freedom alone in a state of rest.

Yet Mazu still spurred Xitang on sternly like this, wanting him to achieve complete mastery of adaptive transformation, without sticking to one corner or getting bogged down in one place.

We must fully comprehend all times past and present and practice harmonious integration, merging into wholeness with no boundaries. It is important in the course of helping people, and receiving oncomers from all sides, that we fish out at least one or two "burnt tails" with the potential to become vessels of the Dharma from within the cave of weeds, people fit to become seedlings of the life of wisdom. Isn't this the work of using expedient means to repay the benevolence and virtue of the buddhas and ancestral teachers?

You must master your spirit, so that whenever you impart some expedient teachings you have the ability in every move to come out with the body of enlightenment and avoid blinding people's eyes. You will do no good if you misunderstand the result and are wrong about the causal basis. This is the most essential path for spiritual friends and teachers.

The great Zen teacher Huinan of Huanglong Temple

once said: "The job of the teacher is to sit upright in the abbot's room and receive all comers with the Fundamental Matter. The other minor business should be entrusted to administrator-monks. Then everything will be accomplished."

How true these words are! When as a Zen teacher you employ people as administrative assistants, you must take great care in entrusting them with appropriate responsibilities, so that affairs will not be mishandled.

Zhenru of Dagui Temple said: "There is no special trick to being a Zen teacher and guiding a community of learners; all that's important is to be skillful in employing people."

Please think this over.

A proverb says: "Cleverness is not as good as a reliable model." Baizhang established a set of guidelines for Zen communities, and no one has ever been able to overthrow them.

Now you should just follow these guidelines conscientiously and take the lead in observing them yourself and do not violate Baizhang's elegant standards. Then everyone in your congregation will follow them too.

In the final breakthrough, a patch-robed monk penetrates through to freedom from death and birth. To succeed at this, you must know the move that a thousand sages cannot trap, the move that cuts off the root of life.

The ancient worthies greatly imbued with the Tao could skillfully capture or release, could skillfully kill or bring life. All the teachers who had attained great liberation used these techniques.

It is not difficult to know about such methods. Whether or not you have mastered them shows up in how you do things. When you can cut through decisively and make them work instantaneously in the situation—only then do you attain power in the long run.

Our ancestral teacher Yangqi spoke of *the diamond cage* and *the thicket of thorns* and used them to distinguish dragons and snakes and capture tigers and rhinos. If you are a genuine descendant of his family, then you will bring them forth at ease and cut off the tongues of Zen monks.

The True School of Linji

The true school of Linji opened its great potential from Linji's great predecessors Mazu and Huangbo, unfurling its great function, escaping all cages, leaving all nests. Charging like tigers and galloping like dragons, flying like shooting stars, striking like lightning, the adepts of the Linji school rolled up and rolled out, captured and released, always employing expedient means based on the Fundamental, always continuous and accurate. When it came to Fengxue and Xinghua, the teaching of the school became more and more lofty, and its workings more and more steep. "West River sports with a lion, frost flowers energize the Diamond King."

No one could have a clue what the Linji school was all about without entering deeply into the inner sanctum and personally receiving the seal and promise of enlightenment. Uninitiated observers just gave their own arbitrary names and descriptions to what they thought they saw, only adding to the foolish word play.

Even having the mettle to storm heaven, and upholding the truth outside conventions, even defeating people's weapons without fighting and killing people without batting an eye—even this does not quite resemble what the Linji school is getting at. Nor for that matter does switching around the constellations and turning the pivot of heaven and the axis of the earth.

Therefore, Linji and his successors taught using such devices as the *three mysteries* and the *three essentials* and the *four perspectives,* and the *four levels of guest and host,* and *the Diamond King's precious sword,* and *the lion crouched to spring,* and *the shout not acting as a shout,* and *the probing pole and the reed shade,* and *distinguishing guest and host and illumination and action in a single shout.* They used so many lines at once! So many scholars have tried to assess these techniques and add explanations, without realizing in the least that their assessments are totally unfounded, because "there is no such blade in our sovereign's armory."

When the adepts of the Linji school bring forth some device for you to see, it happens in the blink of an eye. You must be the superior type of learner who has achieved realization and experiential recognition of the Zen message. Receiving it straight on and bringing it up from the side, you must be a true seedling of the school—how could you depend on intermediaries?

When Baoshou first appeared in his teaching hall, Sansheng pushed a monk forward, and Baoshou immediately hit him. Sansheng said, "If you help people like this, not only have you blinded this monk, but you have blinded the eyes of everyone in the whole city." Baoshou threw down the teacher's staff and returned to his quarters.

Once when Xinghua saw a fellow student approaching, he immediately shouted. The other monk also shouted. Xinghua shouted again. The other monk also shouted again.

Xinghua said, "Look at this blind man!" Then he drove him out of the teaching hall with blows. One of his attendants asked, "What was this monk's offense?" Xinghua said, "He had both the provisional and the real, but I made two passes at him right in front of his face, and yet he didn't understand. If I don't beat a blind guy like this one, when would I ever beat anyone?"

Please observe the true style of the Linji school as it is displayed in these stories. It is absolutely transcendent and does not value any particular strategy. The correctness of one's eye for the Truth is the only thing it considers important.

If you want to uphold the true school and maintain the eye of the Source, you must be completely liberated from head to foot, with a liberation that penetrates the bone and penetrates the marrow and is not entangled with anything whatsoever. Only then can you truly succeed to the Linji school. Only then can you set up the great banner of this teaching and light the great lamp of this teaching. Only then can you continue the work of Mazu and Baizhang and Shoushan and Yangqi without being a usurper.

Transmitting Wisdom

For Buddha's pure transmission on Spirit Peak, for Bodhidharma's secret bequest on Few Houses Mountain, you must stand out beyond categories and apart from conventions and test it in the movements of the windblown dust and grasses.

With your eyes shining bright, you penetrate through obscurities and recognize what is happening on the other side of the mountain. You swallow your sound and eliminate your traces, without leaving behind anything whatsoever. Yet you can set in motion waves that go against the current and employ the ability that cuts off the flow. You go right up to people and nip them. You are swift as a falcon that gets mistaken for a shadow as it soars into the air with its back to the deep blue sky. In the blink of an eye, it's gone. Point to it and it comes. Press it and it goes. It is unstoppably lofty and pure.

This is the way this true source is put into circulation, to serve as a model and standard for later generations. All those who would communicate the message of the source must be able to kill a person's false personality without blinking an eye—only then can they enter into it actively.

One example was old man Huangbo. He knew of this state innately. When he was on his travels, he came to Mount Tiantai, where he saw a saint walking across the waves, cutting off a torrent—Huangbo immediately wanted to strike him dead. When he reached Baizhang and heard the story about how a single shout from Mazu had left Baizhang deaf for three days, he drew back and stuck out his tongue. We know this was the action of Huangbo's great potential. How could those with simplistic opinions and shallow learning form any opinion of it?

Later on Huangbo taught our ancestral teacher Linji and used the whole essence of this. By not holding back his compassion, Huangbo formed Linji into a capable successor who was to give shelter to everyone in the world.

People with the will to reach the Truth must be fully developed and thoroughly polished to make them go beyond conventions and transcend sects. After this they will have the means to *take away the hungry man's food* and *drive off the plowman's ox,* so they can continue the traditional guidance function and not mistake *turning toward* and *turning away.* They can only be seedlings of transcendence when at the subtle level they can see through every drop, and at the expansive level even the thousand sages cannot find them.

Old master Zufeng used to say, "Even Shakyamuni Buddha and Maitreya Buddha are *His* servants. Ultimately, who is *He?*"

How can this admit of arbitrary and confused probing? You will only get anywhere if you know *He* exists.

In general, when as a Zen teacher you would energize the indomitable spirit of a great person in your disciples and make them move ahead into the superior stream, you must set to work and make them so they cannot be trapped and cannot be called back.

As you help people and respond to their potential, it should all be clear and free. You mustn't roll around in the nest of weeds or play with your spirit in the ghost cave. If the supposed teacher uses contrived concepts of "mysteries" and "marvels" and "the essence of truth," if he cocks his eyebrows and puts a gleam in his eye and cavorts around uttering apt sayings and thereby binds the sons and daughters of other people's families with doctrines he claims are absolute realities, then he is just one blind man leading a crowd of blind people—how can this produce any genuine expedient teachings?

Since you already occupy the position of being called a teacher, you certainly cannot take it lightly. For your own part, you must be impeccable, aloof, and transcendent, like a lion on the prowl, with a spirit that frightens the crowd. You must always be unfathomable as you appear and disappear and release and capture. Suddenly, the lion crouches down and springs forward, and all the other animals scatter in a panic. Isn't this especially extraordinary?

If you are such a person, then you have already discerned the outline of this from three thousand miles away. That is why Yantou said: "An enlightened teacher is like a gourd on the water, floating free and at ease, who cannot be reined in or tied down."

When you make contact with Truth, then it covers heaven and earth. Always nurturing it and putting it into practice, you arrive at this stage. Only then do you have a share in the one line that comes from Spirit Peak and Few Houses Mountain. Only then can you take turns as guest and host with Huangbo, Linji, Yantou, and Xuefeng. Only then will your teaching be effective, so that "when the wind moves, the grasses bend down"—and you will not have appeared in the world as a Zen teacher in vain.

Uphold and disseminate the Dharma for twenty or thirty years, and then among the others there will naturally be those who can share in the stream of this realization with you, people of learning and perception who will join you in protecting it.

Who says that no one perceives "the priceless pearl"? I say the black dragon's pearl shines forth wherever it is.

Preparing Successors

The buddhas and ancestral teachers transmitted mind by mind. In this transmission, teacher and disciple were both supremely enlightened. Both had penetrated through to liberation, and so they acted like two mirrors reflecting each other. This is not something that words and images can capture.

When you far transcend all patterns and assessments, and the arrow points meet, without ever having any objective other than Truth, then you receive the marvel of the Way, become a successor of the ancestral teachers, and continue the transmission of the Lamp. You cut off the path of ideation and go beyond thinking and escape from emotional consciousness, to reach a clear, open state of freedom that sweeps all before it.

When it comes time to select people to whom you will impart the bequest, it is necessary to pick those of unique spirit whose enlightened perception is fully mature. Then they will not let the family reputation decline, and they will attain the teeth and claws that have always marked the Zen school since time immemorial. Only then will they be in accord with and truly assist in the transmission of Truth by Truth.

It is by this means that the Zen transmission has continued for many centuries, becoming more and more illustrious the longer it lasts. As the saying goes, "When the source is deep, the stream is long."

Nowadays many have lost the old way, and many try to usurp the style of Zen, setting up their own sects, keeping to clichés, and concocting standardized formulas and slogans. Since they themselves are not out of the rut, when they try to help other people, it is like a rat going into a hollow horn that grows narrower and narrower until the rat is trapped in a total impasse. Under such circumstances, how can the universal teaching not decline?

In the old days, when I first met my teacher Wuzu, I blurted out my realization and presented it to him. It was all words and phrases and intellectual points, all empty talk of "buddhadharma" and "essence of mind" and "mystic marvels."

What I got in return was my old teacher citing a couple of dry phrases: "The verbal and the nonverbal are like vines clinging to a tree." At first I shook this saying back and forth, using my verbal cleverness. Then I began to theorize and expound principles. There were no lengths to which I did not go in the end, as I tried to escape the dilemma he had posed: everything I brought up was included in it. Eventually I began to weep without realizing it. Still, I was never able to get into this saying at all. Again and again I earnestly tried to concentrate on it.

At that point my teacher told me, "You should just put an end to all your arbitrary views and understandings and judgments. When you have cleansed them away all at once, you will naturally gain insight." Then he said, "I have already explained it all for you. Now go."

I sat in my place and investigated the matter thoroughly until there was no seam or gap. Then I went into my teacher's room, and I spoke freely in a confused way. So he scolded me, saying, "Why are you babbling?" At that point I admitted to myself that a man whose eyes were truly clear was seeing into what was in my heart.

In the end, I wasn't able to enter into it, so I left the mountain. Two years later I returned.

Finally, "the bottom fell out of the bucket" for me as I was contemplating the saying: "She calls to her maid again and again, though there's nothing the matter, because she wants her lover to hear her voice." Then at last I saw that what my teacher had told me before was real medicine. It's just that I was deluded at the time and could not penetrate into it.

So I know that the real truth is like Liangsui's saying: "I know everything that you people know, but you people do not know what I know." How true these words are!

Xuefeng asked Deshan, "Do I have any part in the business of the vehicle of the school that has come down from antiquity?" Deshan hit him with his staff and said, "What are you saying?" Later Xuefeng said, "When I was at Deshan's, at a blow from his staff it seemed as if I had stripped off a thousand layers of sweat-soaked shirts clinging to my flesh."

Linji got hit three times by Huangbo and went to Dayu to ask if he was at fault or not. Dayu told him, "Huangbo was so kind to you, but you still come looking for fault." Linji had a powerful realization and unconsciously said, "After all, there's not much to Huangbo's Buddhism."

Both Xuefeng and Linji were outstanding members of the Zen community, and both were enlightened under the impact of a blow from the teacher's staff. Later on they both greatly energized the Zen school and made a ladder and a boat for the salvation of the world. Zen students today should think back on them: were they crude and shallow?

Yet in recent times some people say that using the staff to deal with people is *falling into device and object.* They claim that to enter into the subtle refinements it is necessary to investigate the true nature of mind thoroughly, to discuss mysteries and marvels exhaustively, to be consistent and meticulous at all times, and to pick up every stitch.

But what about all the schools of Buddhism that interpret the scriptural teachings, with their minute analyses, their revelations of hidden aspects, their discovery of ultimate reality and penetration of the true nature of buddhahood? Are these not subtle refinements? If this were all there is to it, then what was the need for the ancestral teacher of Zen to come from the West?

It is evident that since the stream of the Teaching has gone on so long, many divergent views have cropped up. Since they do not get the true transmission, they make the ambrosia of the Buddhist teachings into poison. Is this the fault of Deshan and Xuefeng and Huangbo and Linji?

A proverb says: "If the rope is short, it will not reach far enough to draw water from a deep spring."

Adepts in Action

The Ultimate Path is simple and easy, yet profound and abstruse. From the start it does not set up steps. Standing like a wall miles high, it is called *the fundamental sustenance.*

Thus in Magadha the Buddha carried out the true imperative by shutting his door and staying in seclusion. At Vaishali, Vimalakirta revealed the fundamental principle by keeping his mouth shut and refusing to speak.

Even so, there are adepts who will not forgive them for these displays. How much less would they forgive getting involved with marvels and delving into mysteries, discoursing upon the true nature of mind, and having a sweaty shirt stuck to their skin and being unable to strip it off! That would appear even more broken down and decrepit.

From Bodhidharma to Huineng, the example set by the Zen patriarchs was exceptionally outstanding. The practical strategies of adepts like Linji and Deshan were immediately liberating. When the great Zen masters went into action, they were like dragons galloping and tigers charging: heaven and earth turned, and nothing could stop their revivifying people. They never dragged through the muddy water of emotionalism and intellectualism. Since time immemorial, as soon as they had certain penetration of the ultimate, those with great realization and enlightenment have been like swift falcons and hawks—riding the wind, dazzling in the sun, with the blue sky at their backs.

They penetrated directly through and made themselves completely unobstructed twenty-four hours a day, with their realization pervading everything in all directions, rolling up and rolling out, capturing and releasing. They did not even dwell in the station of sage, so how could they have been willing to remain in the ordinary current? Their hearts were washed clean, and they encompassed both present and past. Picking up a blade of grass, they used it as the golden body of buddha, and picking up the golden body of buddha, they used it as a blade of grass.

For them there was never any such thing as better or worse or grasping and rejecting. They were just vibrantly alive meeting the situation. Sometimes in guiding learners they took away the person but not the world, sometimes they took away the world but not the person, sometimes they took away both, and sometimes they took away neither. They moved beyond conventions and sectarian limits and were totally clear and free. How could they have had any interest in trapping people, in pulling the wool over their eyes, in manipulating them, in bending them out of shape?

It is necessary to get to the reality and reveal to learners the thing in each one of them that is the fundamental matter of great liberation, without dependencies, without contrived activities, without concerns.

This is how the ancients were aware in advance of the dust blowing in the wind and the grasses moving. As soon as any obstructive illusions sprouted, they would immediately mow them down. Still, they could hardly find anybody willing and able to share in the life of wisdom.

How could the genuine Zen teachers be compared with those phonies who roll around in the weeds together, pulling each other along, dragging each other into intellectual and verbal judgments and arbitrary choices, creating clichés to bury the sons and daughters of other people's families? It is obvious that such people are "wetting the bed with their eyes open." Those clear-eyed Zen adepts would never have put on such a display!

The will and energy of the truly great astounds the common herd. You must aim to be their true successor of the genuine school of Linji. With a shout and a blow, an act and a state, face reality and annihilate falsity. Haven't you seen this saying: "Having used the razor-sharp sword of wisdom, be quick to hone it again"?

Move with a Mighty Flow

When your vision penetrates through and your use of it is clear, you are spontaneously able to turn without freezing up or getting stuck amid all kinds of lightning-fast changes and complex interactions and interlocking intricacies. You do not establish any views or keep to any mental states; you move with a mighty flow, so that "when the wind moves, the grasses bend down."

When you enter into enlightenment right where you are, you penetrate to the profoundest source. You cultivate this realization till you attain freedom of mind, harboring nothing in your heart. Here there is no "understanding" to be found, much less "not understanding."

You go on like this twenty-four hours a day, unfettered, free from all bonds. Since from the first you do not keep to subject and object or self and others, how could there be any "buddhadharma"? This is the realm of no mind, no contrived activity, and no concerns. How can this be judged with mere worldly intelligence and knowledge and discrimination and learning, if the fundamental basis is lacking?

Did Bodhidharma actually bring this teaching when he came from the West? All he did was to point out the true nature that each and every person inherently possesses, to enable people to thoroughly emerge clear and pure from the orbit of delusion and not be stained and defiled by all their erroneous knowledge and consciousness and false thoughts and judgments.

"Study must be true study." When you find a genuine teacher of the Way, he will not lead you into a den of weeds; he will cut through directly so you can meet with realization. He will strip off the sweaty shirt that is clinging to your flesh, to enable your heart to become empty and open, without the slightest sense of ordinary and holy, and without any external seeking, so that you become profoundly clear and still and genuine and true. Then even the thousand sages cannot place you. You attain a state that is unified and pure and naked, and pass through to *the other side of the empty aeon.* There even the Primordial Buddha is your descendant, so how could you seek any more from others?

Ever since the ancestral teachers, all the true adepts have been like this. Take the example of the Sixth Patriarch. He was a man from a frontier area in the south who sold firewood for a living, an illiterate. When he met the Fifth Patriarch face to face, he opened his heart and openly passed through to freedom.

The saints and sages live mixed in among the ordinary people, but even so, it is necessary to use appropriate means to reveal this matter that makes no separation between the worthy and the ignorant and is already inherent in all people.

Once you merge your tracks into the stream of Zen, you spend your days silencing your mind and studying with your whole being. You realize that this Great Cause is not obtained from anyone else but is just a matter of taking up the task boldly and strongly, and making constant progress. Day by day you shed your delusions, and day by day you enhance your clarity of mind. Your potential for enlightened perception is like fine gold that is to be refined hundreds and thousands of times. What is essential for getting out of the dusts, what is basic for helping living creatures, is that you must penetrate through freely in all directions and arrive at peace and security free from doubt and attain the stage of great potential and great function.

This work is located precisely in your own inner actions. It is just a matter of being in the midst of the interplay of the myriad causal conditions every day, in the confusion of the red dusts, amid favorable and adverse circumstances and gain and loss, appearing and disappearing in their midst, without being affected and "turned around" by them, but on the contrary, being able to transform them and "turn them around."

When you are leaping with life and water cannot wet you, this is your own measure of power. You reach an empty, solidified silence, but there is no duality between emptiness and form or silence and noise. You equalize all sorts of wondrous sayings and perilous devices and absolute perceptions; ultimately there is no gain or loss, and it is all your own to use.

When you go on "grinding and polishing" like this for a long time, you are liberated right in the midst of birth and death, and you look upon the world's useless reputation and ruinous profit as mere dust in the wind, as a dream, as a magical apparition, as an optical illusion. Set free, you pass through the world. Isn't this what it means to be a great saint who has emerged from the dusts of sensory attachments?

Don't Mix Poison with Your Food

Zhaozhou said, "During my thirty years in the south, the only times I mixed mundane concerns into my mental activity were during the morning and noon meals."

From this we should realize that in carrying out this matter, the ancient worthies did not take it as a casual thing. On the contrary, they took it seriously and treated it with respect. That's how they persevered in their practice and attained insight. That's how they reached thoroughgoing clarity and never fell into empty vanity in action or speech. Thus they managed to unify worldly phenomena and enlightened truth.

In the present time, those who want to draw near to reality must boldly mobilize their energies and transform what is within them. You must not cling to wrong knowledge and wrong views. You must not mix poison into your food. You must be uniformly pure and true and clean and wondrously illuminated to step directly into *the scenery of the fundamental ground* and reach the peaceful and secure stage of great liberation.

Then you stand aloof and alone, so that wind cannot blow in and water cannot wet you. The true essence becomes manifest, and in your daily activities you have a measure of power. As you hear sounds and see forms, you don't give rise to grasping or rejecting. With every move you have a road to get out on.

Haven't you read this story? A monk asked Jiufeng, "I have heard tell that you met Yanshou in person—is this true?" Jiufeng said, "Is the wheat in front of the mountain ripe yet or not?"

If you can recognize what Jiufeng was getting at on the intimate level, you will behold the ability of a true patch-robed monk, what is known as *the sword that kills, the sword that brings life.* Please always keep your eye on this. When you get beyond conventions, then you will naturally know where it's really at.

What Is It?

Zhaozhou said, "I don't like to hear the word *buddha.*"

Tell me, why was he like this? Was it because *buddha* means "omniscient person" that he didn't want to hear the word? Clearly, this was not the reason. Since it wasn't this, then why didn't he want to hear the word? If you are a clear-eyed person, then you'll know where it's really at as soon as you hear of this. Let me ask you: Where is it really at, what does it really mean? Try to divulge what you think about this so I can see.

When Luzu saw a monk coming, he would face the wall—was this helping people or not? Where is the proper proportion? If you want to act in accord with him, what approach should you take?

Every time Baizhang went to the hall, when he had finished expounding the Dharma, and the assembly was dispersing, he would call to them again. When they turned around he would say, "What is it?"

Yaoshan said, "Tell me about what Baizhang used to say as everyone was leaving the hall: whom was it used to contact, and how could insight be attained from it?"

Step Back and Turn to Reality

Gao the patch-robed one,* with his fearless and sharp nature, traveled all over the country visiting the expert craftsmen of the Zen school. The former prime minister and Zen master Zhang Wujin came to know of him and respected him deeply as a vessel of the teaching.

Since Gao had an extraordinary spirit, he was not content to follow small understanding. After demonstrating his sincerity, he became one of my associates. We reached accord at a single word, and he shed the halter that had hitherto bridled

*This was Dahui Zonggao, one of Yuanwu's most illustrious successors, whose own letters and lectures are translated by J. C. Cleary in *Swampland Flowers* (New York: Grove Press, 1978).

him. Though he had still not reached total comprehension, he was a robust and lively fellow whom nobody could suppress or rein in.

When we trace back where this came from, after all it was due to Master Wujin inspiring him. Subsequently Gao braved the freezing cold and came for a while to visit me at Xianping. When he came to announce his departure, he asked for some words of teaching, which I accordingly gave him. This is what I told him:

"Those who wear the patched robe of a Zen wayfarer should be completely serious about taking death and birth as their business. You should work to melt away the obstructions caused by conditioned knowledge and views and interpretive understanding, and penetrate through to a realization of the great causal condition communicated and bequeathed by the buddhas and ancestral teachers. Don't covet name and fame. Step back and turn to reality, until your practical understanding and virtue are fully actualized.

"When there is real attainment, the more you try to hide it, the more it cannot be concealed. All the sages and the *devas* and *nagas* will try to push a person of real attainment forward, especially after years of cultivation and refinement. Wait until you are like a bell sounding when struck or a valley returning an echo. Wait until you are like pure gold coming forth from a forge where it has been smelted and refined ten thousand times, so that it will not change in ten thousand generations, so that it is *ten thousand years in a single moment.*

"When the grip of transcendence is in your hand, when the grasses bend down as the wind blows, then won't you be expansive and generous with resources to spare?

"Remember, what is important in practice is perseverance and consistency."

Kindling the Inexhaustible Lamp

By even speaking a phrase to you, I have already doused you with dirty water. It would be even worse for me to put a twinkle in my eye and raise my eyebrow to you, or rap on the meditation seat or hold up a whisk, or demand, "What is this?" As for shouting and hitting, it's obvious that this is just a pile of bones on level ground.

There are also the type who don't know good from bad and ask questions about Buddha and Dharma and Zen and the Tao. They ask to be helped, they beg to be received, they seek knowledge and sayings and theories relating to the Buddhist teaching and to transcending the world and to accommodating the world. This is washing dirt in mud and washing mud in dirt—when will they ever manage to clear it away?

Some people hear this kind of talk and jump to conclusions, claiming, "I understand! Fundamentally there is nothing to Buddhism—it's there in everybody. As I spend my days eating food and wearing clothes, has there ever been anything lacking?" Then they settle down in the realm of unconcerned ordinariness, far from realizing that nothing like this has ever been part of the real practice of Buddhism.

So we know that you must be someone genuinely within the tradition before you can be fully familiar with the fundamental portion of the vehicle of the school that has come down from time immemorial. If you really have an entry into enlightenment, then you know when to start and when to stop, when to advance and when to withdraw, and you can distinguish what is permissible from what is not.

Leaving behind all leakages, day by day you get closer to the truth and more familiar with it. As you go further, you change like a panther who no longer sticks to its den—you leap out of the corral. Then you no longer doubt all the sayings of the world's enlightened teachers—you are like cast iron. This is precisely the time to apply effort and cultivate practice and nourish your realization.

After that you can kindle the inexhaustible Lamp and travel the unobstructed Path. You relinquish your body and your life to rescue living beings. You enable them to come out of their cages and eliminate their attachments and bonds. You cure them of the diseases of being attached to being enlightened, so that having emerged from the deep pit of liberation, they can become uncontrived, unencumbered, joyfully alive people of the Path.

So then, when you yourself have crossed over, you must not abandon the carrying out of your bodhisattva vows. You must be mindful of saving all beings, and steadfastly endure the attendant hardship and toil, in order to serve as a boat on the ocean of all-knowledge. Only then will you have some accord with the Path.

Don't be a brittle pillar or a feeble lamp. Don't bat around your little clean ball of inner mystical experience. You may have understood for yourself, but what good does it do?

Therefore the ancient worthies necessarily urged people to travel the one road of the bodhisattva path, so they would be able to requite the unrequitable benevolence of our enlightened predecessors who communicated the Dharma to the world.

Nowadays there are many bright Zen monks in various localities who want to pass through directly. Some seek too much and want to understand easily. As soon as they know a little bit about the aim of the Path and how to proceed, they immediately want to show themselves as adepts. Yet they have already missed it and gone wrong. Some don't come forth even when they are pushed to do so, but they too are not yet completely enlightened.

You are a master of Buddhist teaching methods only when you can recognize junctures of times and patterns of causal conditions and manage not to miss real teaching opportunities.

Hidden Treasure

Brave-spirited wearers of the patched robe possess an outstanding, extraordinary aspect. With great determination they give up conventional society. They look upon worldly status and evanescent fame as dust in the wind, as clouds floating by, as echoes in a valley.

Since they already have great faculties and great capacity from the past, they know that this level exists, and they transcend birth and death and move beyond holy and ordinary. This is the indestructible true essence that all the enlightened ones of all times witness, the wondrous mind that alone the generations of enlightened teachers have communicated.

To tread this unique path, to be a fragrant elephant or a

giant, golden-winged bird, it is necessary to charge past the millions of categories and types and fly above them, to cut off the flow and brush against the heavens. How could the enlightened willingly be petty creatures, confined within distinctions of high and low and victory and defeat, trying futilely to make comparative judgments of instantaneous experience, and being utterly turned around by gain and loss?

For this reason, in olden times the people of great enlightenment did not pay attention to trivial matters and did not aspire to the shallow and easily accessible. They aroused their determination to transcend the buddhas and patriarchs. They wanted to bear the heavy responsibility that no one can fully take up, to rescue all living beings, to remove suffering and bring peace, to smash the ignorance and blindness that obstructs the Way. They wanted to break the poisonous arrows of ignorant folly and extract the thorns of arbitrary views from the eye of reality. They wanted to make the scenery of the fundamental ground clear and reveal the original face before the empty aeon.

You should train your mind and value actual practice wholeheartedly, exerting all your power, not shrinking from the cold or the heat. Go to the spot where you meditate and kill your mental monkey and slay your intellectual horse. Make yourself like a dead tree, like a withered stump.

Suddenly you penetrate through—how could it be attained from anyone else? You discover the hidden treasure, you light the lamp in the dark room, you launch the boat across the center of the ford. You experience great liberation, and without producing a single thought, you immediately attain true awakening. Having passed through the gate into the inner truth, you ascend to *the site of universal light.* Then you sit in the impeccably pure supreme seat of the emptiness of all things.

Moving into action as an enlightened teacher, with rolling waves in the ocean of speech, you unleash the skills of unobstructed understanding and eloquence. With chosen pupils you set up a situation or utter a saying to reveal extraordinary perceptions. You cause all beings, whether ordinary or sage, whether sentient or insentient, to look up to the awesome light and receive its protection.

But this is not yet the stage of effortless achievement. You must go further beyond, to where the thousand sages cannot trap you, the myriad conscious beings have no way to look up to you, the gods have no way to offer you flowers, and the demons and outsiders cannot spy on you. You must cast off knowledge and views, discard mysteries and marvels, and abandon all contrived actions. You simply eat when hungry and drink when thirsty, and that's all.

At this stage you are never aware of having mind or not having mind, of gaining mindfulness or losing mindfulness. So how could you still be attached to what you have previously learned and understood, to "mysteries" and "marvels" and analyses of essential nature, to the fetters of names and forms and arbitrary opinions? How could you still be attached to views of "Buddha" and views of "Dharma" or to earth-shaking worldly knowledge and intellect? You would be tying and binding yourself, you would be counting the grains of sand in the ocean—what would there be to rely on?

All those who are truly great must strive to overcome the obstacles of delusion and ignorance. They must strive to jolt the multitudes out of their complacency and to fulfill their own fundamental intent and vows. Only if you do this are you a true person of the Path, without contrived activity and without concerns, a genuine Wayfarer of great mind and great vision and great liberation.

A Lotus in Fire

I wouldn't say that those in recent times who study the Way do not try hard, but often they just memorize Zen stories and try to pass judgment on the ancient and modern Zen masters, picking and choosing among words and phrases, creating complicated rationalizations and learning stale slogans. When will they ever be done with this? If you study Zen like this, all you will get is a collection of worn-out antiques and curios.

When you "seek the source and investigate the fundamental" in this fashion, after all you are just climbing up the pole of your own intellect and imagination. If you don't encounter an adept, if you don't have indomitable will yourself, if you have never stepped back into yourself and worked on your spirit, if you have not cast off all your former and subsequent knowledge and views of surpassing wonder, if you have not directly gotten free of all this and comprehended the causal conditions of *the fundamental great matter*—then that is why you are still only halfway there and are falling behind and cannot distinguish or understand clearly. If you just go on like this, then even if you struggle diligently all your life, you still won't see the fundamental source even in a dream.

This is why the man of old said: "Enlightenment is apart from verbal explanations—there has never been any attainer."

Deshan said: "Our school has no verbal expressions and not a single thing or teaching to give to people."

Zhaozhou said: "I don't like to hear the word *buddha*."

Look at how, in verbally disavowing verbal explanations, they had already scattered dirt and messed people up. If you go on looking for mysteries and marvels in the Zen masters' blows and shouts and facial gestures and glaring looks and physical movements, you will fall even further into the wild foxes' den.

All that is important in this school is that enlightenment be clear and thorough, like *the silver mountain and the iron wall,* towering up solitary and steep, many miles high. Since this realization is as sudden as sparks and lightning, whether or not you try to figure it out, you immediately fall into a pit. That is why since time immemorial the adepts have guarded this one revelation, and all arrived together at the same realization.

Here there is nowhere for you to take hold. Once you can clear up your mind and you are able to abandon all entanglements, and you are cultivating practice relying on an enlightened spiritual friend, it would be really too bad if you weren't patient enough to get to the level where the countless difficulties cannot get near you, and to lay down your body and your mind there and investigate till you penetrate through all the way.

Over thousands of lifetimes and hundreds of aeons up until now, that there ever been any discontinuity in the fundamental reality or not? Since there has been no discontinuity, what birth and death and going and coming is there for you to be in doubt about? Obviously these things belong to the province of causal conditions and have absolutely no connection to the fundamental matter.

My teacher Wuzu often said, "I have been here for five decades, and I have seen thousands and thousands of Zen followers come up to the corner of my meditation seat. They were all just seeking to become buddhas and to expound Buddhism. I have never seen a single genuine wearer of the patched robe."

How true this is! As we observe the present time, even those who expound Buddhism are hard to find—much less any genuine people. The age is in decline and the sages are further and further distant. In the whole great land of China, the lineage of Buddha is dying out right before our very eyes. We may find one person or half a person who is putting the Dharma into practice, but we would not dare to expect them to be like the great exemplars of enlightenment, the "dragons and elephants" of yore.

Nevertheless, if you simply know the procedures and aims of practical application of the Dharma and carry on correctly from beginning to end, you are already producing a lotus from within the fire.

You must put aside all the conditioning that entangles you. Then you will be able to perceive the inner content of the great enlightenment that has come down since ancient times. Be at rest wherever you are, and carry on the secret, closely continuous, intimate-level practice. The *devas* will have no road to strew flowers on, and demons and outsiders will not be able to find your tracks. This is what it means to truly leave home and thoroughly understand oneself.

If, after you have reached this level, circumstances arise as the result of merit that lead you to come forth and extend a hand to communicate enlightenment to others, this would not be inappropriate. As Buddha said, "Just acquiesce in the truth; you surely won't be deceived."

But even for me to speak this way is another case of a man from bandit-land seeing off a thief.

Bringing Out the Family Treasure

If you want to attain Intimacy, the first thing is, don't seek it. If you attain through seeking, you have already fallen into interpretive understanding.

This is especially true because this great treasury extends through all times, clearly evident, empty and bright. Since time without beginning it has been your own basic root: you depend on its power entirely in all your actions.

You will only pass through to freedom when you cease and desist to the point that not even a single thought is born. Then you penetrate through without falling into sense and matter and without dwelling in conceptualizations and mental images.

When you absolutely transcend these, then the whole world does not hide it. Everywhere everything becomes its Great Function, and every single thing flows forth from your own breast. The ancients called this *bringing out the family treasure.* Once this is attained, it is attained forever. How could it ever be used up?

Just be wary that your investigation does not rest on a firm footing, and that you will not be able to penetrate through to realization. You must bravely cut off all entanglements, so there is not the slightest dependence or reliance. Relinquish your body and give up your life and directly accept the suchness that faces you; there is no other. Then even if the thousand sages came forth it wouldn't change you at all. Leaving it to the flow at all times, eating food and wearing clothes, you nurture the embryo of sagehood to maturity, not keeping to intellectual understanding. Isn't this an especially excellent teaching and a most essential shortcut?

A Boatload of Moonlight

The early sages lived with utmost frugality, and the ancient worthies overcame hardships and lived austerely. They purified their *will* in this, forgetting food and sleep. They studied with total concentration and accurate focus, seeking true realization. How could they have been making plans for abundant food and fine clothes and luxurious housing and fancy medicines?

When it gets to the point where the path is not as good as in ancient times, then there is criticism that the wheel of the Dharma is not turning and that the wheel of food is taking precedence. Because of this the Zen monasteries call their chief elders "meal-chiefs." Isn't this completely opposite from the ancient way?

Nevertheless, in the gate of *changing along with conditions,* we also carry out the secondary level. "On the northern mountain welcoming wayfarers from all directions, we look to the southern fields."

This fall it happens that there is a big crop. We have asked you to oversee the harvest, and now that you are about to go, you have asked for some words of instruction, so I have told you about the foregoing set of circumstances.

What is important is to respect the root and extend it to the branches. This will benefit both root and branches and also illuminate the legitimate and fundamental task of people of complete enlightenment and comprehensive mastery. If you work hard to carry this out, you will surely improve.

In general, to study the Path and seek out the Mystery, you must have a great basis in faith. You use this faith to believe in a deep sense that *this matter* does not lie in words or in any of the myriad experiential states. In fact, in truth, the Path is right where you stand.

Put aside the crazy and false mind that has been concocting your knowledge and understanding, and make it so that nothing whatsoever is weighing on your mind. Fully take up *this matter* in your perfect, wondrous, inherent nature, which is fundamentally pure and quiescent. Subject and object are both forgotten, and the road of words and thoughts is cut off. You open through and clearly see your original face. Make it so that once found, it is found forever and remains solid and unmoving.

After that you can change your step and transform your personal existence. You can say things and put forth energy without falling into the realms of the delusions of form, sensation, conception, evaluation, and consciousness. Then all the phenomena of enlightenment will appear before you in regular array. You will reach the state where everything you do while walking and sitting is all Zen. You will shed the root of birth and death and forever leave behind all that covers and binds you. You will become a free and untrammeled wayfarer without concerns—why would you need to search the pages for someone else's dead words?

"There are ancestral teachers on the tips of the hundred

grasses." With these words Jiashan pointed it out so people could become acquainted with it.

Kuanping said, "The great meaning is there in the fields."

Baizhang extended his hands, wanting to let people know.

If you can become round and complete as a ripe grain of rice, this is the transmission of the mind-seal. If you still long for a peaceful existence, this will make you experience the first noble truth that suffering exists. But how will you say something about coming out of the weeds? "A boatload of bright moonlight carries it back."

Truth and Perception

The present perception is the Truth, but the Truth is beyond this perception. If you are attached to perception, then this is a perception—it is not the arriving at the Truth. Those who arrive at Truth transcend perception, but they manage to use perception without dwelling in perception. When you pass directly through perception and get free of it, it is all the fundamental Truth.

This Truth is not being or nonbeing. It is not speech or silence. Yet it can manifest both being and nonbeing, both speech and silence. It is forever constant and unchanging.

Therefore Yunmen said, "It cannot be existent when you speak of it and nonexistent when you don't, or existent when you think of it and nonexistent when you don't."

You must subtly arrive at this Truth and get its great function. Always let transcendent wisdom appear whether you are speaking or silent, whatever you are doing. Is there any need to say that it is close at hand when you are in your teacher's presence and far away when you are in the countryside? As you go directly forward, naturally you will encounter it wherever you are.

All the enlightened ones and ancestral teachers take *this one true thing* very seriously. It is spread among beings of all potentials, high and low, noble and lowly, without any preferences or aversions. It is in all the myriad kinds of action, naturally real, clear and complete.

If you make a special thing out of your views of "buddhadharma" and "mystic marvels," then there is a lack. But if you are able to refrain from creating arbitrary views, and are clean and naked like this, then it is completely revealed.

If this matter were in words, then it should be definable in a single statement, with no further change. Why would there be thousands and thousands of sayings imparted by enlightened adepts, with no end to them? From this we know that it is not within words, but we need to use words to illustrate this matter. Sharp-spirited people should directly comprehend this idea.

Those who realize transcendence pass through words and phrases and can make them come to life. They can use one saying as a hundred thousand sayings or use a hundred thousand sayings as one saying. Why should you have any more doubts about famous Zen sayings like these: "Mind itself is buddha"; "It's not mind, not buddha"; "It's not mind, not buddha, not a thing"; "Mind is not buddha, knowledge is not the Way"; "East Mountain walks on the water"; "Strike the midnight bell at noon"; "A donkey is eating grass in the backyard"; "Hide your body in the Northern Dipper"? All these sayings are strung on one thread.

The venerable Yanyang asked Zhaozhou, "When one

doesn't bring a single thing, then what?" Zhaozhou said, "Put it down." Yanyang asked, "If I don't bring a single thing, what should I put down?" Zhaozhou said, "I see you cannot put it down." At these words, Yanyang was greatly enlightened.

Later Huanglong wrote a verse to go with this story:

Not bringing a single thing
He can't lift it even using both arms
A clear-eyed man like Zhaozhou is hard to find
At a word, Yanyang realized his error
If he stepped back, he'd fall into a deep pit
In his heart was boundless joy
Like that of a pauper finding a jewel
Once the poison is forgotten, there's no
 connection
Snakes and tigers became his intimate friends
Different species, equally understood
Over the lonely centuries,
The Pure Wind has never stopped.

If you discuss Zhaozhou's answer, "Put it down," from the standpoint of common sense, Yanyang said he wasn't bringing a single thing, so how could Zhaozhou tell him to put it down?

From this we know that the eye of objective reality illuminates the finest subtleties: Zhaozhou exposed the serious disease of carrying one's conditioned perceptions around everywhere, to make Yanyang begin to feel shame. But Yanyang still did not realize what Zhaozhou meant, so he persisted with his question. Zhaozhou again pointed out his error, at which point Yanyang dissolved and at last was thoroughly set free. Later on Yanyang got to the point that he could tame wild tigers and poisonous snakes. Isn't this a case of inner feeling and outward response?

Layman Pang was with his whole family sitting around the fire. Layman Pang suddenly said, "Difficult, difficult—ten bushels of oil hemp spread out on a tree." Mrs. Pang said, "Easy, easy—on the tips of the hundred grasses, the meaning of Zen." Their daughter Lingzhao said, "Not difficult, not easy—eating when hungry, sleeping when tired."

Usually when I relate this story to people, most of them prefer Lingzhao's remark for saving energy, and dislike what Old Man Pang and Old Lady Pang said about difficult and easy. This is nothing but "making interpretations by following the words." People who think like this are far from getting to the root of the fundamental design.

That is why "the arising of the tracks of words is the origin of paths that deviate from Truth."

Only if you can *forget the words and embody the meaning* will you see how these three Zen teachers each put forth a hand and together held up the bottomless basket, how they strained out mussels and clams. You will see how in every move they had the ability to kill people's false selves and conditioned perceptions, and how in every place they had a road to get out on.

Direct Pointing

When Bodhidharma came from the West bringing the Zen transmission to China, he didn't set up written or spoken formulations—he only pointed directly to the human mind.

If we speak of *direct pointing,* this just refers to what is inherent in everyone: the whole essence appears responsively from within the shell of ignorance. This is no different in ordinary people than in all the sages since time immemorial. It is what we call the natural, real, inherent nature, fundamentally pure, luminous and sublime. It swallows up and spits out all of space. It is a single solid realm that stands out alone, free of the senses and their objects.

Just detach from thoughts and cut off sentiments and transcend the ordinary conventions. Use your own inherent power and take up its great capacity and great wisdom right where you are. It is like letting go when you are hanging from a mile-high cliff, releasing your body and not relying on anything anymore.

Totally shed the obstructions of views and understanding, so that you are like a person who has *died the great death.* Your breath is cut off, and you arrive at great cessation and great rest on the fundamental ground. Your sense faculties have no inkling of this, and your consciousness and perceptions and sentiments and thoughts do not reach this far.

After that, in the cold ashes of the dead fire, it is clear everywhere, and among the stumps of the dead trees everything is illuminated. Then you merge with solitary transcendence and reach unapproachable heights. You don't have to seek mind or seek buddha anymore: you bump into them wherever you go, and they do not come from outside.

The hundreds and thousands of aspects and facets of enlightenment since time immemorial are just this. This is mind: there is no need to go on seeking mind. This is buddha: why keep struggling to seek buddha?

If you make slogans based on words and sprout interpretations based on objects, then you fall into the bag of antique curios, and you will never be able to find this true realm of absolute awareness beyond sentiments.

At this stage you are free to go forward in the wild field without choosing, picking up whatever comes to hand: the meaning of the ancestral teachers is clear in all that grows there. What's more, the thickets of green bamboo and the masses of yellow flowers and the fences and walls and tiles and pebbles are inanimate things teaching the Dharma. The water birds and the groves of trees expound the truths of suffering, emptiness, and selflessness. Based on the one true reality, they extend objectless compassion, and from the great jewel light of nirvana they reveal uncontrived, surpassingly wondrous powers.

Changqing said, "When you meet a companion on the Path, stand shoulder to shoulder and go on: then your lifetime task of learning will be completed."

Enlightened Reality and Worldly Phenomena

All things are set on a nonabiding basis. The nonabiding basis is based on nonabiding. If you can reach a thorough realization of this, then all things are One Suchness, and you cannot find even the slightest sign of abiding.

The whole of your present activities and behavior is nonabiding. Once the basis is clear to you, it will be like having eyes: the sun is shining brightly, and you can see all kinds of colors and forms. Isn't this the mainspring of transcendent wisdom?

Yongjia said: "Without leaving wherever you are, there is

constant clarity." No words come closer to the truth than these. If you start seeking, then we know that you are unable to see. Just cut off any duality between "wherever you are" and "constant clarity," and make yourself peaceful and serene. Avoid concocting intellectual understanding and seeking. As soon as you seek, it is like grasping at shadows.

Layman Pang asked Mazu, "Who is it that does not keep company with the myriad things?" I say to you: Turn the light around and reflect back on yourself and see.

Mazu replied, "When you drink up all the water in West River in one swallow, then I'll tell you." This answer was like an eight-cornered mortar running through space.

If you can come to grips with this and penetrate through, then what you see before your eyes will reach equilibrium, and the illusions that have afflicted you since time without beginning will be washed away.

Deshan beckoned with a fan from across the river, and someone immediately understood. The Bird's Nest Monk blew on a blanket and someone was enlightened. Doesn't this show that when the time for this Great Cause arrives, the roots and sprouts grow of themselves? Doesn't this confirm that there is space for the teacher's action and the learner's reaction to reach accord? Doesn't this prove that when the people involved have been practicing inwardly, without interruption, they can be activated by a genuine teacher?

When you have complete trust in the mind and you see through to its true nature, then there is not the least bit of leakage in daily activities. The totality of worldly phenomena is the buddhadharma, and the totality of the buddhadharma is worldly phenomena—they are equally One Suchness.

How could it be there when you speak of it and not there

when you don't, or there when you think of it and not there when you don't? If that is so, then you are right there in the midst of false imagination and emotional interpretations—when have you ever experienced penetrating realization?

When there is continuous awareness from mind-moment to mind-moment that does not leave anything out, and mundane reality and enlightened reality are not separate, then you will naturally become pure and fully ripe and meet the Source on all sides. If anyone asks questions, you answer according to the question, and if there are no questions, you remain clear and still. Isn't this the essential guideline for really passing through birth and death to freedom?

When you have passed through the Last Word, then you won't even need to "see through" speech and no-speech, transcendence and accommodation, provisional and real, illumination and function, giving and taking away. Who recognizes the mastery of a great Zen teacher like Zhaozhou? To do this, you must be a seedling of our house.

This Great Cause

In the olden days, whenever teachers and students met, it was for the sake of *this Great Cause,* and they never failed to use it to inspire and uplift. Even when they were eating or sleeping or at leisure, they were always concentrating their minds on this.

That is why they were able to experience a meeting of potentials in a word or a phrase, a blow or a shout, or any momentary event or activity. This was because with sincerity and concentrated focus, and without so much defilement by wrong ideas and perceptions, they were able to take it up directly, and it didn't seem difficult.

These days the brethren are errant and dull and all mixed up with miscellaneous concerns. Even if they study with an enlightened teacher and are exposed to his influences for a long time, they still vacillate and waver and cannot proceed directly to penetrating realization. The problem is the lack of purity and focus over the long term.

If you can work hard on the Way day and night heedless of food and sleep, have no worries that you will not equal the ancients.

Meet the Source on All Sides

Those who are determined to practice the Way practice self-awareness and self-understanding twenty-four hours a day. They think of this and focus on this. They know that *the one Great Cause* is there right where they stand, that it is in sages without being augmented and in ordinary people without being diminished. They know that it stands alone free of senses and sense objects, and that it far transcends material things.

Wayfarers don't set up fixed locations in anything they do. They are clear and tranquil, with solid concentration, and the myriad changes and transformations never disturb them. They appear in response to conditions and go into action as they encounter events, leaving nothing incomplete.

You should just be empty and quiet, transcending everything. Once the main basis is clear, all obscurities are illuminated. *"Ten thousand years—a single thought. A single thought—ten thousand years."* Passing through from the heights to the depths, the great function of the whole potential is in operation. It is like when a strong man flexes his arm: he doesn't depend on anyone else's strength. Then the illusory blinders of birth and death vanish forever, and the true essence indestructible as a diamond is all that shows. Once realized, it is realized forever—there is no interruption.

All that the enlightened teachers, ancient and modern, have said and done—the scriptural teachings, the enlightenment stories, the meditation stories, the question-and-answer sessions, all their teaching functions—all of this illuminates this true essence alone.

If you can be free and clear in actual practice for a long time, naturally you will come to meet the Source on all sides and become unified and whole.

Haven't you seen Fadeng's verse?

Going into a wild field, not choosing,
Picking up whatever plant comes to hand,
Rootless but finding life,
Apart from the ground but not falling.

Right before your eyes, it has always been there. Facing the situation, why don't you speak?

If you don't know it in your daily life, where then will you look for it? Better find out.

Truly Genuine

Right now if students are in fact truly genuine, source teachers can contact their potential and activate it with a single word or phrase, or a single act or scene. What could be difficult about that?

The only problem is when your faculties are unstable and your consciousness shallow, whirled around and around like the wind in the treetops. True reality is shown to you thousands and thousands of times, but you still cannot mesh with it.

Even worse are those who are still wrapped up in making emotional interpretations and claim that there is no such thing as entry into enlightenment. If you think like this, then even in a blue moon you will never even dream of true reality.

Therefore, in learning the Way, what is most valuable is being true and sincere.

Serene and Free

People who study the Way begin by having the faith to turn toward it. They are fed up with the vexations and filth of the world and are always afraid they will not be able to find a road of entry into the Way.

Once you have been directed by a teacher or else discovered on your own the *originally inherently complete real mind,* then no matter what situations or circumstances you encounter, you know for yourself where it's really at.

But then if you hold fast to that real mind, the problem is you cannot get out, and it becomes a nest. You set up "illumination" and "function" in acts and states, snort and clap and glare and raise your eyebrows, deliberately putting on a scene.

When you meet a genuine expert of the school again, he removes all this knowledge and understanding for you, so you can merge directly with realization of the original uncontrived, unpreoccupied, unminding state. After this you will feel shame and repentance and know to cease and desist. You will proceed to vanish utterly, so that not even the sages can find you arising anywhere, much less anyone else.

That is why Yantou said, "Those people who actually realize it just keep serene and free at all times, without cravings, without dependence." Isn't this the door to peace and happiness?

In olden times Guanxi went to Moshan. Moshan asked him, "Where have you just come from?" Guanxi said, "From the mouth of the road." Moshan said, "Why didn't you cover it?" Guanxi had no reply.

The next day Guanxi asked, "What is the realm of Mount Moshan like?" Moshan said, "The peak doesn't show." Guanxi asked: "What is the man on the mountain like?" Moshan said, "Not any characteristics like male or female." Guanxi said, "Why don't you transform?" Moshan said, "I'm not a spirit or a ghost—what would I transform?"

Weren't the Zen adepts in these stories treading on the ground of reality and reaching the level where one stands like a wall miles high?

Thus it is said: "At the Last Word, you finally reach the impenetrable barrier. Holding the essential crossing, you let neither holy nor ordinary pass."

Since the ancients were like this, how can it be that we modern people are lacking?

Luckily, there is the indestructible diamond sword of wisdom. You must meet someone who knows it intimately, and then you can bring it out.

Active Meditation

The ancients worked hard for the sake of *the one Great Cause.* Their determination is indeed worthy of respect, and they served as an everlasting example for later generations.

When you set your body on the meditation bench, it is no more than silencing and emptying the mind and investigating with your whole being. Just make your mind and thoughts clarify and become still. A fine place to do active meditation work is amid confusion and disturbances. When you do active meditation, you must penetrate through the heights and the depths, without omitting anything. The whole essential being appears ready-made before you, and it no longer arises from anywhere else. It is just this *one Great Potential,* turning smoothly and steadily. Why talk any more about "worldly phenomena" and "enlightened truth"? If you maintain a uniform equilibrium over months and years, naturally your stand will be true and solid.

You will experience realization, like water being poured into water, like gold being traded for gold. Everything will be equalized in One Suchness, profoundly clear, real, and pure. This is knowing how to live.

Just do not give birth to a single thought: let go and

become crystal clear. As soon as any notions of right and wrong and self and others and gain and loss are present, do not follow them off. Then you will be personally studying with your own true enlightened teacher.

If you do that, what worry is there that this work will not be accomplished? You must see for yourself!

How to Be a Householder-Bodhisattva

This affair is a matter of people of sharp faculties and superior wisdom who do not consider it difficult to understand a thousand when hearing one. It requires a stand that is solid and true and faith that is thoroughgoing.

Then you can hold fast and act the master and take all sorts of adverse and favorable situations and differing circumstances and fuse them into one whole—a whole that is like empty space, without the least obstruction, profoundly clear and empty and illuminated, never changing even in a hundred aeons or a thousand lifetimes, unitary from beginning to end. Only then do you find peace and tranquillity.

I have seen many people who are intellectually brilliant but whose faculties are unstable and whose practice is shallow. They think they witness transformation in verbal statements, and they assume that there is no way to go beyond the worldly. Thus they increase the thorns of arbitrary opinion as they show off their ability and understanding. They take advantage of their verbal agility and think that the buddhadharma is like this. When situations are born from causal conditions, they cannot pass through to freedom, so they wind up vacillating back and forth. This is really a great pity!

This is why the ancients went through all sorts of experiences and faced all sorts of demons and difficulties. They might be cut to pieces, but they never gave it a thought; they took charge of their minds all the way along and made them as strong as iron or stone. Thus when it came to passing through birth and death, they didn't waste any effort. Isn't this where the special strength and generosity beyond emotionalism that truly great people possess lies?

When bodhisattvas who live a householder's life cultivate the practices of home-leavers, it is like a lotus blooming in fire. It will always be hard to tame the will for fame and rank and power and position, not to mention all the myriad starting points of vexation and turmoil associated with the burning house of worldly existence. The only way is for you yourself to realize your fundamental, real, wondrous wholeness and reach the stage of great calm and stability and rest.

It would be best if you managed to cast off everything and be empty and ordinary. Thoroughly experience the absence of conditioned mind, and observe that all phenomena are like dreams and magical illusions. Be empty all the way through, and continue on clearing out your mind according to the time and the situation. Then you will have the same correct foundation as all the great enlightened laymen in Buddhist tradition.

According to your own measure of power, you will transform those not yet enlightened so you can enter together into the uncontrived, uncluttered ocean of true nature. Then your life here on this earth will not be a loss.

It Doesn't Come from Outside

The essential thing in studying the Way is to make the roots deep and the stem strong. Be aware of where you really are twenty-four hours a day. You must be most attentive. When nothing at all gets on your mind, it all merges harmoniously, without boundaries—the whole thing is empty and still, and there is no more doubt or hesitation in anything you do. This is called the fundamental matter appearing ready-made.

As soon as you give rise to the slightest bit of dualistic perception or arbitrary understanding and you want to take charge of this fundamental matter and act the master, then you immediately fall into the realm of the clusters of form, sensation, conception, value synthesis, and consciousness. You are entrapped by seeing, hearing, feeling, and knowing, by gain and loss and right and wrong. You are half drunk and half sober and unable to clean all this up.

Frankly speaking, you simply must manage to keep concentrating even in the midst of clamor and tumult, acting as though there were not a single thing happening, penetrating all the way through from the heights to the depths. You must become perfectly complete, without any shapes or forms at all, without wasting effort, yet not inhibited from acting. Whether you speak or stay silent, whether you get up or lie down, it is never anyone else.

If you become aware of getting at all stuck or blocked, this is all false thought at work. Make yourself completely untrammeled, like empty space, like a clear mirror on its stand, like the rising sun lighting up the sky. Moving or still, going or coming, it doesn't come from outside. Let go and make yourself independent and free, not being bound by things and not seeking to escape from things. From beginning to end, fuse everything into one whole. Where has there ever been any separate worldly phenomenon apart from the buddhadharma, or any separate buddhadharma apart from worldly phenomena?

This is why the founder of Zen pointed directly to the human mind. This is why *The Diamond Sutra* taught the importance of human beings detaching from forms. When a strong man moves his arm, he does not depend on someone else's strength—that's what it's like to be detached from forms.

To develop this essential insight, it is best to spend a long time going back into yourself and investigating with your whole being, so that you can arrive at the stage of the genuine experience of enlightenment. This is what it means to study with boundless, infinite enlightened teachers everywhere in every moment.

Strive sincerely for true faith, and apply yourself diligently to your meditation work. This is the best course for you.

Abandoning Entanglements

Yantou said, "Abandoning things is superior, pursuing things is inferior." If your own state is empty and tranquil, perfectly illuminated and silently shining, then you will be able to confront whatever circumstances impinge on you with the indestructible sword of wisdom and cut everything off—everything from the myriad entangling objects to the verbal teachings of the past and present. Then your awesome, chilling spirit cuts off everything, and everything retreats of itself without having to be pushed away. Isn't this what it means to be well endowed and have plenty to spare?

If the basis you establish is not clear, if you are the least bit bogged down in hesitation and doubt, then you will be dragged off by entangling conditions, and obviously you will not be able to separate yourself from them. How can you avoid being turned around by other things? When you are following other things, you will never have any freedom.

The Ultimate Path is simple and easy—it is just a matter of whether you abandon things or pursue them. Those who would experience the Path should think deeply on this.

People in ancient times gave up their whole bodies for the sake of this one matter. They stood out in the snow, worked as rice pounders, sold off their hearts and livers, burned their arms, threw themselves into roaring fires, got dismembered and cut to pieces, fed themselves to tigers and birds of prey, gave away their heads and eyes, endured a thousand kinds of pain and suffering.

In sum, if you do not suffer hardship, you will not arrive at deep realization. Those with the will for the Path must certainly consider the ancients as their comrades and aspire to equal their standard.

Meeting It Wherever You Touch

Round and clear, empty and still—such is the essence of the Way. Extending and withdrawing, killing and bringing life—such is its marvelous function.

When you are able to travel on the sword's edge, when you are able to persevere and hold on, when you are like a pearl rolling around in a bowl, like a bowl rolling a pearl around inside it, when you never fall into empty vanity even for an instant, when you never divide worldly phenomena from the buddhadharma but fuse them into one whole—this is called *meeting it wherever you touch.* You appear and disappear and move freely in all directions, and there is never anything external. You are clean and naked, turning smoothly, sealing everything with the fundamental. It is clear everywhere, complete in everything—when has there ever been gain and loss or affirmation and denial or good and evil or long and short?

Your only fear should be that your own correct eye is not yet perfectly clear. This will cause you to fall into duality, and then you will lose touch with reality. Haven't you read what Yongjia said? "The top-flight people have one decisive realization and comprehend all. With people of the middling and lower sort, the more they hear, the more they don't believe."

Words and Truth

The verbal teachings of the buddhas and ancestral teachers are just a snare and a trap. They are used as a means of entry into truth. Once you have opened through into clear enlightenment and taken it up, then in the true essence, everything is complete. Then you look upon all the verbal teachings of the buddhas and ancestral teachers as belonging to the realm of shadows and echoes, so you never carry them around in your head.

Many students in recent times do not get to the basis of the fundamental design of the Zen school. They just hold onto the words and phrases, trying to choose among them, discussing how close or how far away they are from the truth, and distinguishing gain and loss. They interpret fleeting provisional teachings as real doctrines and boast about how many koans they have been able to sift through and how well they can ask questions about the sayings of the Five Houses of Zen. They are totally sunk in emotional consciousness, and they have lost the true essence in their delusions. This is truly a pitiful situation!

A genuine Zen teacher would use any means necessary to warn them of their error and enable them to get away from all such wrong knowledge and wrong views. But they would reject this—they would call it contrived mental activity to turn people around and shake them up and refine them. Thus they enter ever more deeply into the forest of thorns of erroneous views.

As the saying goes, "In the end, if you do not meet an adept, as you get older you will just become a fossil."

You must not depend on either the pure or the impure.

Having mind and having no mind, having views and having no views—both alternatives vanish like a snowflake put on a red-hot stove. Twenty-four hours a day, from top to bottom, you are free and untrammeled as you wander this road that the thousand sages do not share. Just bring this to complete purity and ripeness and you will naturally become a real person, beyond study and free from contrived activity, a real person whom thousands and tens of thousands of people cannot trap or cage.

The Gate Beyond

Where is it that you are walking? If you knew all about the currents as you sailed the boat and could tell the waves apart as you plied the oars, then what need would there be to go to such lengths to admonish and instruct you? You could reach complete comprehension at one stroke.

Thus, the wind blows and lightning flashes—if you hesitate, you are a thousand miles away. This Zen teaching is only for receiving the swift, not for the ignorant. That is why in Zen we say, "We cast our hook into the four oceans, just to catch fierce dragons. The mysterious device beyond conventions is just to seek out those who know."

Once you have arrived in Zen, as you observe all in the world and beyond the world, there has never been any change: you see through everything from top to bottom. Then you know how to relinquish your body and your life, and in the midst of all kinds of different situations, you will be calm and unmoved. You will always be equanimous, even if you meet the power of the wind of objects, and you will always be at ease, even if you are doused with poison.

If you do not continue to practice and nurture and develop this for a long time, then how can you hold up the sun and the moon of the buddhadharma with great insight and great illumination, appearing and disappearing freely? There has never been any turning toward or turning away with this stage: you must open up the gate beyond.

Walking on the Ground of Reality

For the sake of this Great Teaching, the ancients gave up their bodies and their lives and endured endless immeasurable hardship and toil, until they thoroughly clarified its profound essential message. They treasured it like a precious jewel and guarded it like their eyes. They worked on it assiduously and never let it be taken lightly or defiled.

As soon as the slightest trace of special understanding arises, it is like clouds casting a pall over a clear sky, like dust obscuring the surface of a mirror.

Thus Zhaozhou said, "When I was in the south, for thirty years, except at mealtimes, I never used my mind in a way that mixed in worldly concerns."

Caoshan instructed people to guard this matter as carefully as if they were passing through a village with poisoned wells and could not let a single drop of the poisoned water touch them.

By forgetting conditioned mind and cutting off conditioned awareness, you arrive in practice at the true realm of

Thusness. There is nothing on your mind and no mind on things: you are equanimous and free from contrived actions, transcendent as you move on alone.

Only when you yourself walk upon the ground of reality can you help people by dissolving sticking points and removing bonds. You liberate everyone, even though there is really no one to liberate.

You must put the Last Word to use—then you will have a way out everywhere in everything.

Always Mindful

The ancients were always mindful of *this matter.* Whether deep in the mountain valleys or in the bustling villages and towns, they never turned their backs on it for an instant. Whatever scenes or circumstances they encountered, amidst sound and form, in the course of movement and action, they invariably turned around and focused back on their own true selves. The practice of all the adepts since time immemorial who completely penetrated through was none other than this.

Thus, with their fundamental basis firm and strong, they were not blown around following the wind of objects. They were serene and at peace and did not fall into the scope of feelings of holy and ordinary. They came directly to great cessation and great rest: they "found the seat and put on the robe."

Now you are returning to your home village, able to see as the ancients saw. If you can make it continuous and unbroken, how will it be any different than when you were in the monastery being guided by the abbot and doing your meditation work? If you turn your back on it at all, and there is some break in the continuity, then you will lose contact.

We are about to part, so remember these words. Another time in the future, don't look back and blame me for not admonishing you.

Be Undefinable

For students of mystic wisdom, seeing the real nature of things and awakening to the true pattern and treading in the steps of the buddhas is everyday food and drink.

You should realize that on the crown of the heads of the buddhas and enlightened adepts there is a wondrous way of "changing the bones" and transforming your existence. Only then can you get beyond conventional categories and sectarian limits and act like a transcendent person, so that even great Zen masters like Linji and Deshan would have no way to apply their blows and shouts to you.

At all times just remain free and uninvolved. Never make any displays of clever tricks—be like a stolid simpleton in a village of three families. Then the gods will have no road on which to offer you flowers, and demons and outsiders will not be able to spy on you.

Be undefinable, and do not reveal any conspicuous signs of your special attainment. It should be as if you are there among myriad precious goods locked up securely and deeply hidden in a treasure house. With your face smeared with mud and ashes, join in the work of the common laborers, neither speaking out nor thinking.

Live your whole life so that no one can figure you out, while your spirit and mind are at peace. Isn't this what it is to be imbued with the Way without any contrived or forced actions, a genuinely unconcerned person?

Among the enlightened adepts, being able to speak the Truth has nothing to do with the tongue, and being able to talk about the Dharma is not a matter of words.

Clearly we know that the words spoken by the ancients were not meant to be passively depended on. Anything the ancients said was intended only so that people would directly experience the fundamental reality. Thus, the teachings of the sutras are like a finger pointing to the moon, and the sayings of the Zen masters are like a piece of tile used to knock on a door.

If you know this, then rest. If your practice is continuous and meticulous and your application broad and all-pervading, and you do not deviate from this over the years, then you will mature in your ability to handle the teachings, to gather up and to release, and you will be able to see through petty things and cut them off without leaving a trace.

Then when you come to the juncture of death and birth, where all the lines intersect, you won't get mixed up. You will be clear and immovable, and you will be set free as you leave this life behind. This is deathbed Zen, for the last day of your life.

Completing the Task

Awakening on your own without a teacher, *before the Primordial Buddha,* you proceed straight to transcendent realization, on the same road as the thousand sages. You are able to let go and act freely, able to hold fast and be absolutely still, able to act the master. The Whole appears before you in all its completeness—without needing to be refined, it naturally becomes pure and ripe.

When it comes to *after the Primordial Buddha,* though you have your own independence which you directly accept to arrive at the stage where there is no doubt, you still should rely on a teacher to make sure and to approve your enlightenment and make you into a vessel of the Teaching. Otherwise, there are sure to be demons who will malevolently ruin the correct basis.

For this reason, ever since the ancestral teachers, the apprentice receives and the teacher transmits, and the teacher's teaching is of the utmost value. This is especially true with *this matter,* which is not something that can be comprehended by worldly intelligence or confined within perception and knowledge.

Unless you have the bold, fierce spirit of a person of power, and manage to select a genuine enlightened teacher as your spiritual friend, how can you cut off the flow of birth and death and break out of the shell of ignorance?

If you investigate and inquire diligently for a long time with singleminded concentration, the time of fruition will come—suddenly the bottom drops out of the bucket and you will empty out and awaken to enlightenment. After that, you work wholeheartedly to weed out what's wrong and make sure of what's right, for experiential proof of your realization. Then it will naturally be like a boat going downstream—no need to work at rowing. This is the true meeting of teacher and disciple.

Once you have attained the essential gist of the teaching, concentrate continuously so there are no breaks or interruptions, to enable the embryo of sagehood to grow and mature. Then even if you encounter bad conditions, you will be able to melt them away with true insight and the power of concentration, and fuse everything into one whole, so the great changes of birth and death will not be enough to disturb your heart.

Nurturing your enlightenment over many years, you become a greatly liberated person who is free from contrived actions and obsessive concerns. Isn't this what it is to have accomplished what was to be done and completed the task of travel?

Out and Back

This matter lies in the swiftness and sharpness of the person involved. Once you have taken it up and put it into practice, and you know you have your own place to stand, you should be aloof and independent—stand alone and go alone. You should cut off sentiments and detach from perception and make yourself empty and silent so there is not a single thing that can be grasped. Cut off the myriad entanglements, and make yourself free and untrammeled, and reach the stage of great peace. When this is closely continuous without any leaks, this is what is called standing like a wall miles high, lofty and steep.

After that you come back to the world and respond to beings. Since there is never any sense of self, how could there be any realms of sound and form, of adversity and ease, of delusion and enlightenment?

What is most difficult is to be perfectly at rest, not activating the conceptual faculty. If you are suddenly dragged off by it, you have leaked and tarried. You must continue to concentrate so that your mind does not wander off. After a long time it will fuse into one whole. This at last is where you find rest.

From here you must still go on to master transcendent action. An ancient worthy said, "Find the seat and put on the robe, and afterward see for yourself."

Washed Clean

In visiting enlightened teachers and questioning them, you must see real nature and awaken to truth. As you directly forget feelings and put an end to views, you are inwardly washed clean. You become like a simpleton, not calculating gain and loss, not contending for superiority. Favorable or adverse, you cut everything off and don't let it continue. After a long time at this, you naturally arrive at the stage where there are no contrived activities and no concerns.

As soon as you have the slightest wish to be unconcerned, a concern has already arisen. Once one wave goes into motion, myriad waves follow—when will it ever stop? When death comes upon you in that condition, you will be frantic and confused, simply because you are not free and clear.

Just make this work sure and true, and naturally even in a noisy marketplace it will be silent and still as water. Why worry then that you will not accomplish your task?

"As soon as there is affirmation and negation, the mind is lost in confusion." How many people have been started by this statement into making judgments and arguments! If you cut them off at the start, you penetrate through to the other side of the Primordial Buddha. If you follow these words along, you'll be even more confused. To get it, you have to turn your own light around and look back.

Self and Things

All the myriad things are neither opposed to nor contrary to your true self. Directly pass through to freedom and they make one whole. It has been this way from time without beginning.

The only problem is when people put themselves in opposition to it and spurn it and impose orientations of grasping or rejecting, creating a concern where there is none. This is precisely why they are not joyfully alive.

If you can cut off outward clinging to objects and inwardly forget your false ideas of self, things themselves are the true self, and the true self itself is things: things and true self are one suchness, opening through to infinity.

Then at all times, whatever you may be doing, it stands like a mile-high wall—where is all the trouble and disturbance?

Time and again I see longtime Zen students who have been freezing their spirits and letting their perception settle out and clarify for a long time. Though they have entered the Way, they immediately accepted a single device or a single state, and now they rigidly hold to it and won't allow it to be stripped away. This is truly a serious disease.

To succeed it is necessary to melt and let go and spontaneously attain a state of great rest.

The Secret Seal

Here at my place there is no Zen to explain and no Path to transmit. Though five hundred patch-robed ones are gathered together here, I just use *the diamond trap* and *the thicket of thorns.* Those who leap out of the diamond trap make an effort to leap out, those who swallow the thicket of thorns swallow it with care. Don't be surprised that they have no flavor or that they are dangerous and steep.

If you suddenly attain realization, it is like returning to your native village in broad daylight dressed in brocade: everyone will look up to you in admiration.

In essence, you cannot find where this one comes from: it's called the fundamental matter that is inherent in everyone. As soon as you deliberately intend to accept it or take it up, this is already not the fundamental anymore. Just get the myriad impulses to cease, so even the thousand sages do not accompany you—then how could there still be any dependency?

You should put everything aside right away and penetrate through to freedom on that side. That is why it is said, "Even the slightest thing is dust—as soon as you rouse your intellect you are assailed by the demons of delusion."

Forming all things just depends on *that;* destroying all things also just depends on *that.*

What should be formed and perfected? The causal conditions of special excellence, the treasury of merits and virtues countless as the sands, the countless wondrous adornments and world-transcending rarities.

What should be destroyed and obliterated? Greed and anger and jealousy, emotional consciousness and attachments, contrived actions and defiled actions, filth and confusion, names and forms and the interpretive route, arbitrary views and knowledge and false sentiments.

That can transform all things, but nothing can transform *that.* Though it has no shape or visage, it contains all of space. It contains the ordinary and nurtures the holy. If you try to grasp it through forms, then in grasping at it you fall into the thorns of views, and you will never ever find it.

It was just this wondrous mind that the buddhas revealed and the ancestral teachers directly pointed out. When you take it up directly, without producing a single thought, and penetrate from the heights to the depths, everything appears ready-made. Here where it appears ready-made, you do not exert any mental effort: you go along freely with the natural flow, without any grasping or rejecting. This is the real esoteric seal.

Bearing this esoteric seal is like carrying a lamp hidden in the darkness as you roam through the world without longing or fear—it is all the realm of your own great liberation, continuing forever without interruption.

That is why it is said that the sixteen-foot golden body of buddha functions as a blade of grass, and a blade of grass functions as the sixteen-foot golden body of buddha. How could there be anything else?

This Side and That Side

You came to my room and asked about the issues you have doubts about. You said, "In this one matter, why do Zen teachers often speak to people of 'this side' and 'That Side'?" So I spoke to you about this.

Cutting directly through based on the fundamental, how could there be any such plurality? Yet the Zen teachers imparted various expedient teachings and provisional techniques for the purpose of helping people enter into the experience of the Way. Thus they imposed this division into "this side" and "That Side," though there is actually no duality.

Haven't you seen this story? A monk asked Caoshan, "The ancients upheld 'That Side.' How would you have me approach it?" Caoshan said, "Step back to your true self and you won't miss anything." On hearing this, the monk had an insight.

This is what is called *recognizing the intent on the hook* that the teacher uses to "fish" for the student's true potential and *not accepting the marks on the scale* of a provisional definition as an absolute standard.

You must reach the limit of the present time, then you can take up the transcendent matter. But how will you manage to reach the limit of the present time? You yourself must be quick to apply your energies, slough off entangling sense objects, and make your heat free and clear. Not establishing anything, you penetrate through from top to bottom and become open and empty and still. Don't try to interpret this as some extraordinary experience. Just wait till you reach accord with the fundamental, and you will naturally realize enlightenment on your own and reach the realm of great peace.

How can this be conveyed in words on paper? Please try to see it with your own eyes.

Total Peace

The wondrous path of the enlightened ones is straight and direct. They just pointed directly to the human mind so we would work to see its true nature and achieve enlightenment.

This mind-source is originally empty and peaceful, clear and wondrous, and free from the slightest obstruction. But we screen it off with false thoughts and give rise to defilements and blockages in this unobstructed one. We turn our backs on the fundamental and pursue the trivial and foolishly revolve in the cycle of routine.

If you have great capacity, you won't seek outside anymore. Right where you stand you will come forth in independent realization. When the transitory blinders of false perception have been dissolved away, the original correct perception is complete and wondrous. This is called the identity of mind and buddha.

From this, once realized, it is realized forever. It is like the bottom falling out of a bucket: you open through and merge with the Way, and there is nothing occupying your mind. Beholding the essence, pure and still, you receive the use of it and have no more doubts. Then when one is comprehended, all are comprehended.

When you hear it said that "it is not mind, not buddha," when you encounter situations favorable or unfavorable, good or bad, you seal it fast with one seal. How could there be any self or others, any same or different? How could there be so many kinds of mixed-up knowledge and views?

Thus the ancient worthies achieved sincerity and entered truth with every act and every state, with every word and every silence. A thousand methods, ten thousand doors—ultimately there is no difference. It is like hundreds and thousands of different streams all returning to the great ocean.

Once you spontaneously abide at peace in this, and can put it to use in a thoroughgoing, penetrating way, then you are a person of the Path who has nothing more to learn, free from contrived activities and obsessive concerns. Twenty-four hours a day you do not engender any other states of mind or give rise to any divergent views. You eat and drink and dress according to the occasion. You are empty and solid in all situations, and you will never waver, even in a thousand years.

When you are in this state of great concentration, isn't this inconceivable great liberation? Just let it continue for a long time without interruption. Do not fall into "inner" and "outer" and "in-between." Do not fall into being and nothingness, into defiled and pure. Cease and desist straightaway. When you see buddhas and sentient beings as equal and no different, this at last is the stage of total peace and bliss.

Now that you have the right orientation, it is just a matter of nurturing it and making it pure and ripe. Keep on refining and perfecting it. Only when you are like fine gold that has been smelted a hundred times can you become a great vessel of the Teaching.

Entering the Path

The Tao is originally without words, but we use words to reveal the Tao. People who truly embody the Tao penetrate it in the mind and clarify it at its very basis. They strip off thousands and thousands of layers of sweaty shirts sticking to their skin and open through to awaken to the real, true, immutable essence, which is just as it is: originally real and pure and luminous and wondrous, wholly empty and utterly silent.

When you reach the point where not a single thought is born and before and after are cut off, you walk upon the scenery of the fundamental ground. All the wrong perceptions and wrong views of self and others and "is" and "is not" that make up the defiled mind of birth and death are no longer there. You are completely cleansed and purified, and you have complete certainty. Then you are no different from all the other enlightened people since time immemorial.

You are at peace, not fabricating anything, not clinging to anything, freely pervading everything by being empty, perfectly fused with everything, without boundaries. You eat and dress according to the time and season and have the integral realization of true normality. This is what it means to be a true nondoing, unaffected Wayfarer.

In sum, it depends on the fundamental basis being illuminated and the six sense faculties being pure and still. Knowledge and truth merge, and mind and objects join. There is no profundity to be considered deep and no marvel to be considered wondrous. When it comes to practical application, you naturally know how to harmonize with everything. This is called "finding the seat and putting on the robe."

After this you see on your own. You never consent to bury yourself at the verbal level in the public cases of the ancients or to make your living in the ghost cave or under the black mountain. The only thing you consider essential is enlightenment and deep realization. You naturally arrive at the stage of unaffected ordinariness, which is the ultimate in simplicity and ease. But you never agree to sit there as though dead, falling into the realm of nothingness and unconcern.

This is why, in all the teaching methods they employed, the enlightened adepts since antiquity thought the only important thing was for the people being taught to stand out alive and independent, so that ten thousand people couldn't trap them, and to realize that the vehicle of the school of transcendence does actually exist.

The enlightened adepts never ever made rigid dogmatic definitions, thereby digging pitfalls to bury people in. Anyone who does anything like this is certainly playing with mud pies—he is not someone who has boldly passed through to freedom, not someone who truly has the enlightened eye.

Therefore, we do not eat other people's leftovers by accepting stale formulas and worn-out clichés, for to do so would mean being tied up to a hitching post for donkeys. Not only would this bury the Zen style; it would also mean being unable to penetrate through birth and death oneself. Even worse would be to hand on slogans and clichés and subjective interpretations to future students and to become one blind person leading a crowd of blind people and proceeding together into a fiery pit.

Do you think this would be only a minor calamity? It would cause the true religion to weaken and fade, and make the comprehensive teaching design of the enlightened ancestors collapse. How painful that would be!

Therefore, in studying the Tao, the first requirement is to select a teacher with true knowledge and correct insight. After that, you put down your baggage and, without any question of how long it will take, you work continuously and carefully on this task. Don't be afraid that it is difficult and painful and hard to get into. Just keep boring in—you must penetrate through completely.

Haven't you see Muzhou's saying? "If you haven't gained entry, you must gain entry. Once you have gained entry, don't turn your back on your old teacher."

When you manage to work sincerely and preserve your wholeness for a long time, and you go through a tremendous process of smelting and forging and refining and polishing in the furnace of a true teacher, you grow nearer and more familiar day by day, and your state becomes secure and continuous.

Keep working like this, maintaining your focus for a long time still, to make your realization of enlightenment unbroken from beginning to end. The things of the world and the buddhadharma are fused into one whole. Everywhere in everything you have a way out—you do not fall into objects and states or get turned around by anything.

At a bustling crossroads in the marketplace, amid the endless waves of life—this is exactly the right place to exert effort.

Joyously Alive

The essential requirement in studying Zen is concentrated focus. You don't engage in any forced actions: you just keep to the Fundamental. Right where you stand, you must pass through to freedom. You must see the original face and walk through the scenery of the fundamental ground. You do not change your ordinary actions, yet outside and inside are One Suchness. You act according to the natural flow and do not set up anything as particularly special—you are no different from an ordinary person.

This is called being a Wayfarer who is free and at peace, beyond learning, free from contrived actions. Being in this stage, you do not reveal any traces of mind—there is no road for the gods to offer you flowers, and no way for demons and outsiders to spy on you. This at last is simple unadorned reality.

Keep on nurturing this for a long time, and worldly phenomena and the buddhadharma fuse into one whole, merging without boundaries. Power functions ready-made, so what is so difficult about penetrating through birth and death to freedom?

The only worry is that your initial realization will not be accurate and true. If there is anything in your breast, then you're hung up and blocked. If you want to *reach accord* quickly, you must dissolve everything as soon as it happens, like a snowflake placed on a red-hot stove. Then you will naturally open through and become peaceful and still and attain great liberation.

Step back yourself and examine this. You have associated with a teacher for quite a while already, so ask yourself if your practice is reaching the right outcome or not. If it is coming down in the right place, then what are you still in doubt about?

From now on, do not give rise to a single thought, and accept true reality with your whole body. If you are real in one place, then how could it be any different in a thousand or ten thousand places?

The ancestral teachers just wanted people to see their true nature. All the enlightened ones came forth to enable people to awaken to mind. Once you arrive at the reality of mind and its true nature, and it is pure and unified and unmixed with deluded perceptions, then the four elements that make up your physical body, and the five clusters of form, sensation, conception, evaluative synthesis, and consciousness, and the six sense faculties and the six sense objects, and all the myriad forms of being together comprise the place where you relinquish your body and your life.

When you are at peace and washed clean, it is like the sun shining everywhere, like the infinite expanse of space. How can you confine yourself to your limited body and mind and keep yourself from being joyously alive?

People of olden times would spend ten or twenty years studying just to penetrate through. And after they penetrated through, they knew how to live.

Are people these days lacking anything to keep them from proceeding along the same path? Just don't give rise to any feelings of wanting or needing anything, or engender any clingings or attachments. Then, according to your power as you encounter situations, you will not fail to penetrate through.

All that's important is concentrated focus, purity, and stillness. Even when you are engaged in doing things, this is not something external. Take hold of them and return them to your true self—this is what *wondrous function* is. The eighty thousand sensory afflictions are immediately transformed into eighty thousand means of transcendence, and there is no more need to make a special point of studying with teachers. In your daily activities you deliver countless numbers of sentient beings and accomplish countless enlightening works and pass through countless gates of the Dharma. It all flows out from within your own breast—how could there be any other?

As the saying goes: "From atop the hundred-foot-high pole, you must take a step forward—then the universe in all its multiplicity reveals the whole body of reality."

Now Is the Time

To study the Path you should step back and study with your whole being. Make birth and death your only thought. The worldly truth is impermanent, this body is not everlasting. Once you stop breathing, then it's already another lifetime. In another birth you may sink into nonhuman species, and then you might go on for thousands of lifetimes through countless ages without emerging.

Luckily, at present you still have plenty of time. Now is the time to apply effort to turn toward the Path every moment, without your mind wavering or your attention faltering. Catch sight of it right where you are. When you reach the point where not a single thought is born and before and after are cut off, you will suddenly penetrate through to freedom. It's like the bottom falling out of a bucket. Then you experience joy.

You investigate into the ultimate depths until you walk in

the scenery of the fundamental ground and clearly see *the original face.* Then you will have no more doubts about what the Zen masters have said. You will be able to cut everything off and hold everything still, nurturing it by having no conditioned mind and no contrived effort and no particular concerns. Then twenty-four hours a day, there will be no more wasted effort. Your mind does not touch upon things and your steps are beyond location.

At this point you are a true Zen monk who has understood things and completed the work. You do not aim to get famous or play false to grasp at profit. You stand like a wall miles high—impeccable, with "each drop of water a drop of ice." You work on your own mission of getting beyond birth and death and pay no attention to anything else. Not disturbing anything in the realm of sound and form, not startling the everyday people, you go freely into independent liberation and become a true saint who has gone beyond the dusts.

You must have faith in this and put it into practice.

Leaping Out of the Pit

Since ancient times we have only esteemed forgetting thoughts and feelings and finding independent realization. Once getting this realization, we do not set up the idea of self, and we do not congratulate ourselves or put on lofty airs. We just go along freely according to the natural flow, like know-nothings, like simpletons. Only this can be called the practice of a nonstriving, unconcerned person of the Path.

If you can go on like this for three or four or five decades without changing or deviating, then it will also be *thus,* being as it is, for a thousand lifetimes and ten thousand aeons. As the saying goes, "Hardest of all to find are people who will persevere forever." If you go on consistently like this, fully believing, completely penetrating through, have no worries that you will be unable to cross over the world and leap out of the pit of the afflictions of birth and death.

It is just a matter of the person concerned having faculties that are bold and sharp—then it wouldn't be considered difficult even to transcend the cosmic buddha Vairocana or go beyond all the generations of ancestral teachers. This is the real gate of great liberation.

When Bodhidharma passed on the Zen teaching to his successor Huike, was he bogged down in so many verbal explanations?

You must comprehend directly, penetrating from the heights to the depths without the slightest deviation, so that apparent reality cannot break you and the myriad impulses cannot get to you. After that you let everything flow forth from the nonabiding basis in unhindered harmony. All activities are just one's own wondrous function. Wherever you are, you pull out nails and extract wedges for people and enable each of them to become peaceful and secure. Isn't this what's most essential?

One day Xuansha saw some men carrying a corpse. He pointed to this and said to his companions, "Four dead men are carrying one live one." According to the conventional view, Xuansha got it backward. If you use the true eye of transcendence to detach from subjective views and go beyond conventional sentiments, then you will know that Xuansha was being extremely kind in helping people.

Therefore, to pass through to freedom, you must get beyond the nexus of form, sensation, conception, motivational synthesis, and consciousness.

Haven't you read the ancient worthy's saying? "The white clouds are clear and still, and the rivers flow into the blue sea. The myriad things are originally peaceful, but people make trouble for themselves."

After all, this statement is completely accurate and true. If you know what it means as soon as you hear it mentioned, you can use it to pass through birth and death to freedom and no longer be obstructed by the psycho-physical nexus. You will be like a bird getting out of a cage—independent and free. With a single stroke you put a stop to all other actions and talk, and you no longer fall into secondary views.

Enlightenment Right Where You Stand

Among the marvels of Buddhism, nothing surpasses the Zen school for experiencing direct surpassing realization and reaching quick accord with transcendent wisdom. This is the pure, clean Zen of the supreme vehicle of those who come from Thusness.

It has been specially carried on outside of doctrine ever since Shakyamuni Buddha held up a flower on Spirit Peak and Mahakashyapa smiled—Shakyamuni entrusted to him the wondrous mind of nirvana, the treasury of the eye of the correct teaching. The pure transmission of the mind-seal continued through twenty-seven generations in India, until bodhidharma came from the West to bring it to China. He pointed directly to the human mind, to enable people to see their true nature and become enlightened, regardless of whether they are ordinary or sagely or far or near.

When the basic capacity is attuned, you pass through to freedom in an instant. It doesn't take three incalculable aeons: you immediately witness the original buddha, which is perfect and complete and pure and wondrous.

Therefore, to travel in the Zen school, you need a great capacity for the Dharma. You must establish your determination from the start and set out: then you must come forth transcendent. This is what is called realizing buddhahood right where you stand. Reining in your thoughts and concentrating your awareness for a while, you no longer set up "before" and "after"—you experience the unborn.

This is not obtained from anyone else. It is just a matter of bold and sharp practice on your own part. It is like cutting through a skein of thread: when one thread is cut, they are all cut. Your inherent spiritual awareness is instantly liberated: one moment you're an ordinary person, and the next moment you're a sage. Whether you intend it or not, the ordinary and the sagely are One Suchness, embracing all of space, with no more direction or location.

Yongjia said: "How can you draw any comparisons to the uncreated state of absolute reality? Transcend directly to enter into the stage of those who realize Thusness."

At the assembly where Buddha preached *The Lotus Sutra,* a *naga* girl offered a pearl and immediately achieved true awakening. Isn't this immediate realization of the wondrous fruit of enlightenment in the turn of a thought?

This reality cannot be covered by the skies or held up by the earth. Space cannot contain it. It abides within all sentient beings and is the support on which all of them rest. It has always been clean and naked. There is nowhere it does not pervade.

People are unable to experience this true essence simply because they are hemmed in by emotional consciousness and separated from it by hearing and seeing, and because they falsely accept the perceived reflections of objects for mind itself and the gross physical elements as the real body.

That is why the sages, with the power of their vows of compassion, have pointed out this true essence to people, to enable all people with the basic capacity to turn the light around and reflect back, so they can pick it out and witness it in its pure form.

How about the "pearl" that the *naga* girl offered to Buddha—where is it right now? If you can take it up as soon as it's mentioned, then you will never go to the words to construct an understanding, or make a nest in mental maneuvers and conceptual thoughts. Then it will be no different from the undefiled world of Spirit Peak.

Since time immemorial we in the Zen school have only valued the very first mental moment, the very first statement. Before thought is born, before sound comes forth, cut through directly—all at once cut off the spiritual workings of the thousand sages and the spiritual talisman of the myriad sentient beings. Isn't this the essential wondrous realm of liberation and freedom, where you achieve great independence?

Layman Pang asked Mazu, "Who is the one who does not keep company with the myriad things?" Mazu said, "When you can swallow all the water in West River in one gulp, I'll tell you."

Many are the people who make verbal evaluations of this

public case, interpreting it in terms of mind and environment, but they are far from accepting the design of Zen.

You have to be made of cast iron: only then can you go against the flow and experience transcendent realization. Then you will capsize the iron boat of Layman Pang and Mazu. When you arrive at last at *towering up like a wall miles high,* you will finally know that there aren't so many things.

Time Waits for No One

All those with conditioned minds are as far apart from true reality as the sky is from the earth. Right now, if you cannot pass through the barrier, it is obviously because your mind has many serious attachments. If you can clear these away and reach the realm where there is no conditioned mind, all delusions and defilements and emotional habits will end, and all the obstructions created by conditioned knowledge and arbitrary views and intellectual understanding will be dissolved away—what else is there?

This is why Nanquan said that, once freed from its conditioning, the ordinary mind is the Way. But as soon as you produce a thought seeking to be "ordinary," you have already turned away and missed it. This is the point that is most subtle and hardest to approach. Even immeasurably great people falter and hesitate when they get here—how much the more so for those still in the stage of learning.

You must strive with all your might to bite through here and cut off conditioned habits of mind. Be like a person who has *died the great death:* after your breath is cut off, then you come back to life. Only then do you realize that it is as open as empty space. Only then do you reach the point where your feet are walking on the ground of reality.

When you experience profound realization of this matter, you become thoroughly clear, and your faith becomes complete. You are free and at ease and clean clear through—not knowing anything, not understanding anything. As soon as anything touches you, you turn freely, with no more constraints, and without getting put anywhere. When you want to act, you act, and when you want to go, you go. There is no more gain or loss or affirmation or denial. You encompass everything from top to bottom all at once.

How could it be easy to carry into practice or even to approach this realm where there is no conditioned mind? You must be a suitable person to do so. If you are not yet like this, you must put aside mind and body and immerse yourself in silent reflection until you are free from the slightest dependency. Keep watching, watching, as you come and go. After a long time you will naturally come to cover heaven and earth, so that true reality appears ready-made wherever you touch.

Before there was a natural-born Shakyamuni Buddha, before there was a spontaneously so Maitreya Buddha, who was it who understood while still in the womb? You must be quick to focus your energy. Time does not wait for people. Suddenly, in one bite, you will bite through, and nobody will be able to do anything about you. To succeed at this, a truly great person must reach the realm of self-realization, independence, and freedom.

Make Enlightenment Your Standard

Fundamentally, this great light is there with each and every person right where they stand—empty clear through, spiritually aware, all-pervasive, it is called *the scenery of the fundamental ground.*

Sentient beings and buddhas are both inherently equipped with it. It is perfectly fluid and boundless, fusing everything within it. It is within your own heart and is the basis of your physical body and of the five clusters of form, sensation, conception, motivational synthesis, and consciousness. It has never been defiled or stained, and its fundamental nature is still and silent.

False thoughts suddenly arise and cover it over and block it off and confine it within the six sense faculties and sense objects. Sense faculties and sense objects are paired off, and you get stuck and begin clinging and getting attached. You grasp at all the various objects and scenes, and produce all sorts of false thoughts, and sink down into the toils of birth and death, unable to gain liberation.

All the buddhas and ancestral teachers awakened to this true source and penetrated clear through to the fundamental basis. They took pity on all the sentient beings sunk in the cycle of birth and death and were inspired by great compassion, so they appeared in the world precisely for this reason. It was also for this reason that Bodhidharma came from the West with the special practice outside of doctrine.

The most important thing is for people of great faculties and sharp wisdom to turn the light of mind around and shine back and clearly awaken to this mind before a single thought is born. This mind can produce all world-transcending and worldly phenomena. When it is forever stamped with enlightenment, your inner heart is independent and transcendent and brimming over with life. As soon as you rouse your conditioned mind and set errant thoughts moving, then you have obscured this fundamental clarity.

If you want to pass through easily and directly right now, just let your body and mind become thoroughly empty, so it is vacant and silent yet aware and luminous. Inwardly, forget all your conceptions of self, and outwardly, cut off all sensory defilements. When inside and outside are clear all the way through, there is just one true reality. Then eyes, ears, nose, tongue, body, and conceptual mind, form, sound, smell, flavor, touch, and conceptualized phenomena—all of these are established based on that one reality. This one reality stands free of and transcends all the myriad entangling phenomena. The myriad phenomena have never had any fixed characteristics—they are all transformations based on this light.

If you can trust in this oneness, then with one comprehended, all are comprehended, and with one illuminated, all are illuminated. Then in whatever you do, it can all be the indestructible true essence of great liberation from top to bottom.

You must awaken to this mind first, and afterward cultivate all forms of good. Haven't you seen this story? The renowned poet Bo Juyi asked the Bird's Nest Monk, "What is the Way?" The Bird's Nest Monk said, "Don't do any evils, do all forms of good." Bo Juyi said, "Even a three-year-old could say this." The Bird's Nest Monk said, "Though a three-year-old might be able to say it, an eighty-year-old might not be able to carry it out."

Thus we must search out our faults and cultivate practice;

this is like the eyes and the feet depending on each other. If you are able to refrain from doing any evil and refine your practice of the many forms of good, even if you only uphold the elementary forms of discipline and virtue, you will be able to avoid sinking down to the levels of animals, hungry ghosts, and hell-beings. This is even more true if you first awaken to the indestructible essence of the wondrous, illuminated true mind and after that cultivate practice to the best of your ability and carry out all the forms of virtuous conduct.

Let no one be deluded about cause and effect. You must realize that the causal basis of hell and heaven is all formed by your own inherent mind.

You must keep this mind balanced and equanimous, without deluded ideas of self and others, without arbitrary loves and hates, without grasping or rejecting, without notions of gain and loss. Go on gradually nurturing this for a long time, perhaps twenty or thirty years. Whether you encounter favorable or adverse conditions, do not retreat or regress—then when you come to the juncture between life and death, you will naturally be set free and not be afraid. As the saying goes, "Truth requires sudden awakening, but the phenomenal level calls for gradual cultivation."

I often see those who are trying to study Buddhism just use their worldly intelligence to sift among the verbal teachings of the buddhas and ancestral teachers, trying to pick out especially wondrous sayings to use as conversation pieces to display their ability and understanding. This is not the correct view of the matter. You must abandon your worldly mentality and sit quietly with mind silent. Forget entangling causes and investigate with your whole being. When you are thoroughly clear, then whatever you bring forth from your own inexhaustible treasury of priceless jewels is sure to be genuine and real.

So first you must awaken to the Fundamental and clearly see the true essence where mind equals buddha. Detach from all false entanglements and become free and clean. After that, respectfully practice all forms of good, and arouse great compassion to bring benefits to all sentient beings. In all that you do, be even and balanced and attuned to the inherent equality of all things—be selfless and have no attachments. When wondrous wisdom manifests itself and you penetrate through to the basic essence, all your deeds will be wonder-working. Thus it is said, "Just manage to accept the truth—you won't be deceived."

Make enlightenment your standard, and don't feel bad if it is slow in coming. Take care!

The Original Person

The Great Teaching is basically quite ordinary. It is easy to enter for those with sharp faculties and quick wits and broad penetration who don't use their intellectual brilliance to try to comprehend it.

The usual problem is if you are overloaded with conditioned knowledge and arbitrary views. Then when you try to approach this source, the more you delve into it, the farther away you get, and you are completely unable to penetrate through.

If you are equanimous toward everything, including the ultimate ungraspability of mind itself, and your conditioned mind fades away and spontaneously comes to an end, then the perfect illumination of inherent nature appears whole without needing any contrived efforts to make it. You cut off the flow and experience profound realization. When you neither go too far nor fail to go far enough, then you arrive at the naturally real working essence of the mind. This is what is meant by the saying, "Set to work on mind, and the matter is decided." If you always let this naturally real essence appear amidst your daily activities, then how can you not be settled and secure?

When the ancients awakened to mind, they awakened to this mind. When they activated its working potential, they activated this working potential. They were able to stay free and at ease for ten thousand generations without changing. They stood forth transcendent, in independent realization, and no longer placed themselves in opposition to anything.

If you are in opposition to anything, then this creates duality. Then you are stuck with self and others and gain and loss, and you are unable to walk upon the ground of reality.

If you take a step further, not a single thing is established—after that you are quiet and properly attuned, and you clearly see the original person. You get rid of all the concerns in your breast and the mental moment that's before your eyes, so that your whole being is liberated and at peace. You are forever beyond any possibility of retreating or regressing. You attain fearlessness, and with expedient means based on this fearlessness, you can rescue sentient beings.

You must continue this way without interruption forever—this is the best.

Witnessing the Tao

This Tao is deep and remote. Beyond the time before heaven and earth had taken shape and sentient beings and buddhas were separated, it was profoundly clear, solid and still, as the root of the myriad transformations. From the beginning it was never existent or nonexistent and never fell into the dusty realm of sensory objects. This Tao shines and glitters, and none can fathom its limits. It has no reality that can be considered real and no wonder that can be considered wondrous. It is absolutely transcendent and lies beyond the scope of concepts and images. There is nothing that can be used to compare it with.

Therefore, the perfected people witness it independently and come forth liberated. They are annihilated and totally cleansed, and they penetrate through to this primal source.

By the power of expedient means, these perfected people bring it up directly in its pure form, to receive students of the highest potential without establishing any steps or stages. This is why their teaching is called *the vehicle of the source,* and *the special practice outside doctrines.* They seal qualified disciples with this one seal. In turning the key of transcendence, there is no room for hesitation in thought.

In all the methods and gestures they use, the enlightened teachers leave behind the nests of cliché and theory and verbal sloganeering. They are like sparks struck from stone, like flashes of lightning—instantaneous, swift. They produce thousands of changes and transformations without ever depending on anything. From top to bottom they cut through the net that traps people. They sanction only the outstanding students and disregard the dullards.

To be a legitimate Zen teacher, you must have the spirit to kill a person's false personality in the blink of an eye. Understanding one, you understand all; illuminating one, you illuminate all. After that you arrive at the far-seeing perception and lofty consciousness that comes with getting beyond birth and death and transcending ordinary life and entering into the bequest of the sages. You live in an ordinary way and do not reveal your sharp point. When you suddenly come forth free and at ease, you startle the multitude and move the crowd.

In sum, your roots are deep and your stem is strong. You see that *before the Primordial Buddha* and *the other side of the empty aeon* are no different from your functioning here and now. Once your practice has power, you are able to bear the heavy responsibility of teaching the Dharma and achieve far-reaching effects—you achieve great mastery. Then compressing three aeons into a single moment or stretching out seven days into a whole age is just minor action—to say nothing of taking the galaxy and hurling it beyond space, or putting the polar mountain into a mustard seed. This is your everyday food and drink.

In the past there were many examples of enlightened lay people who combined worldly achievement with profound mystic realization. It wasn't so hard—all they did was directly comprehend this one Great Cause. Once they had this Tao as their foundation, they were able to disregard other people's conventional judgments and mobilize their own courage and boldness. When interacting with people, they focused the eye of enlightenment and set in motion their quick potential and sharp wisdom to turn all the myriad forms of being around, back into their own grasp. They rolled out and they rolled up, they released and they captured. Thus they were no different from all the people of great attainment down through the ages whose practice was pure and ripe and who held within them the virtues and power of the Tao.

Just make the transmission continue without a break from source to source, and then you will be a joyously alive person on the road of eternal life.

The ancestral teacher said: "Mind turns following the myriad objects. If you can really reach the hidden depths of this turning and recognize true nature going along with the flow, then there is no joy and no sorrow." As soon as you can find the deep meaning in this transformation process, you will penetrate through the moving flow and see inherent true nature. When you move beyond duality and do not abide in the middle path, how can there still be any such things as adverse and favorable, sorrow and joy, or love and hate to block your free functioning?

To transmit mind by means of mind, to seal true nature with true nature—this is like water being poured into water, like trading gold for gold. Joyous, easy, ordinary, without contrived activity, without concerns—as you meet situations and circumstances, they are not worth a push.

Are the direct teaching methods of the classic Zen masters so remote? Just do not let yourself be transformed by following your emotions. Get above form and ride upon sound. Transcend ancient and modern. Move quickly on the razor's edge amidst the multiplicity.

Thus it is said, "Push open the passageway to transcendence, and all the thousand sages are downwind of you."

Right in Your Own Life

This thing is there with everyone right where they stand. But only if you have planted deep and strong roots in the past will you have the strength in the midst of the worldly truth to be able to push entangling objects away.

You must constantly step back from conventional perceptions and worldly entanglements to move along on your own and reflect with an independent awareness. Cleanse and purify your karma of mind, body, and mouth, sit upright and investigate reality, until you arrive at subtle insight and clear liberation.

Right in your own life, detach from conditioned views and cut off sentiments. Stand like a wall a mile high. Abandon the deep-seated conditioning and the erroneous perception that has been with you since time without beginning. Smash the mountain of self to pieces, dry up views based on craving, and directly take up the truth. The thousand sages cannot alter it, and the myriad forms cannot cover it or hide it. It lights up the heaven and the earth.

The buddhas and ancestral teachers pointed directly to this indestructible, inherent true essence, which is wondrous, immaculate, and pure. Set your eyes on it amid the thousands of intricate complexities that are impossible to analyze. Apply your blade where the interlocking crosscurrents cannot be split apart.

Your potential operates prior to things, and your words go beyond the scope of concepts. You are free and unbound, pure and still. You turn independently, with your powerful functioning alive and liberated. You share the same attainment and the same functioning with all the outstanding adepts since antiquity who have achieved this realization—you are not different, not separate. Unoccupied and at ease, you just preserve stillness and silence and never show your sharp point. You seem like a simpleton, totally abandoned and relaxed, eating when hungry and drinking when thirsty, no different than usual. This is what is called secretly manifesting the great function and activating the great potential without startling the crowd.

When you have done this for a long time and arrived at the stage where you are pure and ripe and at peace and genuine, is there any more old bric-a-brac like affliction and birth and death that can tie you down?

Therefore, those among the ancients who were adept in the Way and its powers directed people who had already freed themselves from sensory entanglements to extend the esoteric seal.

You should spend twenty or thirty years doing dispassionate and tranquil meditation work, sweeping away any conditioned knowledge and interpretive understanding as soon as it arises, and not letting the traces of the sweeping itself remain either. Let go on That Side, abandon your whole body, and go on rigorously correcting yourself until you attain great joyous life. The only fear is that in knowing about this strategy, the very act of knowing will lead to disaster. Only when you proceed like this will it be real and genuine practice.

Haven't you read of all the Zen masters who emphatically praised the state where there is no conditioned mind? They really wanted future learners to proceed like this. If you make a display of your cleverness and verbal analyses and intellectual understanding, you are polluting the mind ground, and you will never be able to enter the stream of the Way. Many people have tried to spin out rationales to explain why Buddha held up the flower on Spirit Peak and why Bodhidharma sat facing a wall at Shaolin, but they do not rely on the fundamental. They are far from realizing that searching for the meaning of the mind-to-mind transmission through verbal categories and sound and form is like sticking your head into a bowl of glue.

As for the outstanding type, they certainly do not act like this. They are able to delve into it on their own and are sure to get the sense of the great and far-reaching acts of the classic teachers. They discover the real truth by engaging with it. That is why people of attainment do not even have any spare time to wipe their noses.

But tell me, where were the ancestral teachers of Zen operating? It's evident that the unique transmission outside of doctrine was not a hurried undertaking. They looked to the void and traced its outline: each and every one penetrated through from the heights to the depths and covered heaven and earth. They were like lions roaming at ease, sovereign and free. When they were empty and open, they really were empty and open, and when they were close and continuous, they really were close and continuous.

Although it is just this one thing that we all stand on, ultimately you yourself must mobilize and focus your energy. Only then will you really receive the use of it.

Entering the Path

The subtle wondrous Path of the buddhas and enlightened teachers is nowhere else but in the fundamental basis of each and every person. It is really not apart from the fundamentally pure, wondrously illuminated, uncontrived, unconcerned mind.

If you have sincerely devoted yourself to it for a long time, yet are still not able to become really genuine, it is because you have been trying to approach it via your intellectual nature and its many machinations.

You should simply make this mind empty and unoccupied and quiet and still. If you continue in a state of profound stillness and harmony with reality as it is for a long time without changing or shifting, there is sure to come a day when you enjoy total peace and bliss.

What you should worry about is that you will be unable to stop and will go on seeking outside yourself with your intellect. Little do you realize that the real nature you inherently possess is hard and solid as a diamond, secure and everlasting. It is just a matter of never letting there be even a moment's interruption in your awareness of your real nature.

If you put your conditioned intellect to rest for a long time, suddenly it will be like the bottom falling out of a bucket—then you will naturally be happy and at peace. If you seek teachers and insist on memorizing a lot of their instructions, you are even further off. What you must do is use your bold basic nature and boldly cut off and abandon your conditioned mind—you are sure to experience the Path and know it for yourself.

After you know you have entered the Path, you do not set up even this "knowing"—then you arrive at last at the realm of true purity.

The Inexhaustible Treasury

Devas and humans and all sentient beings, including the enlightened ones, all depend on the awesome power of this thing.

But although ordinary sentient beings have this within them, they are in the dark about it, and so they become wrongly subject to sinking down into the cycle of birth and death and affliction.

The enlightened ones, on the other hand, arrive at the awesome power of this thing and thus experience transcendent realization.

Though delusion and enlightenment differ, their underlying inconceivable reality is one and the same.

That is why the buddhas and ancestral teachers gave instructions and pointed directly to this reality. They always directed sentient beings to comprehend for themselves their own inherent, fundamental, perfect, wondrously illuminated true mind and to dispense with all the false thoughts and schemes and knowledge and views associated with sensory afflictions and troubles.

Go directly to your personal existence in the field of the five clusters of form, sensation, conception, motivational synthesis, and consciousness, turn the light around and reflect back. Your true nature is clear and still and as-is—empty through and accept it. When you clearly see this true nature, this true nature *is* mind, and this mind *is* true nature. All activities, all the myriad changes and transformations in the sensory realm, have never shaken it. That is why it is called the ever-abiding fundamental source.

If you reach this basic root, whatever you do in your empowered functioning will penetrate through. What is necessary is to cut off the flow of your conditioned mind and witness it. If you hesitate in thought, then you are out of touch. If a person's root nature has been pure and still and settled for a long time, it is very easy to be empowered—just reflect back a bit, and penetrate through, and then you can witness it and experience entry.

The ancients called this *the inexhaustible treasury* and also *the wish-granting jewel* and also *the indestructible precious sword.* You must have deep roots of faith and believe that this is not gotten from anyone else.

Whether you are walking, standing, sitting, or lying down, concentrate your spirit and silently reflect. Be pure and naked, without interruptions and without breaks, so that naturally no subjective views arise, and you will merge with this true essence. It is neither born nor destroyed, neither existent nor nonexistent. It is neither solid nor empty; it is apart from names and forms. This is the scenery of your own fundamental ground, your own original face.

When the ancients employed all their hundreds and thousands and millions of expedient teaching devices, it was always to enable people to go toward this and penetrate through to freedom. As soon as you penetrate through, then you penetrate through deeply to the source. You cast aside the tile that was used to knock at the gate, the provisional means that were used to get you there, and there is absolutely nothing occupying your feelings.

Actually practice at this level for twenty or thirty years and cut off all the verbal demonstrations and creeping vines and useless devices and states, until you are set free from conditioned mind. Then this will be the place of peace and bliss where you stop and rest.

Thus it is said: "If you are stopping now, then stop. If you seek a time when you finish, there will never be a time when you finish."

Simple and Easy

"The wonders of the Path are as simple and easy as can be." How true these words are! But those who have not reached the source think that the Path is extremely abstruse and mysterious. They think that the ultimate reality of the Path lies before the empty aeon, before the differentiation of the primeval chaos, before heaven and earth were formed. They think it is something silent and dark and vague, something impossible to fully fathom or investigate or probe, and that only the sages can experience or know it. Thus they know the words of the sages, but they do not know their meaning. How can we talk to them about this matter?

People who think like this are far from realizing that the Path is perfect and complete right under everyone's feet, that it is pure and naked in the midst of everyday activities. It encompasses all mental moments and is omnipresent in all places.

There is no dark place it does not illuminate and no time it is not in operation.

It is just that people have been running off in the opposite direction for a long time, branching off in aberrant ways, unwilling to believe in their own buddha nature, always seeking externally—that is why the more they seek, the further away they get from the Path.

This is why Bodhidharma came from the West and just pointed directly to the human mind. This mind is the unconcerned mind in its normal equilibrium. Its natural potential spontaneously extends forth, without constraints and without clinging, without abiding anywhere or getting attached to anything. It shares in the powers of heaven and earth and merges with the light of the sun and moon.

There is no room here to set up arbitrary opinions. You flood out into great comprehension and merge into a state free from conditioned mind and its contrived actions and obsessive concerns. If you set up the slightest trace of dualism between subject and object and self and others, then you are blocked off and obstructed, and you will never penetrate through to it.

As the saying goes: "The real nature of ignorance is buddha nature, and the empty body of illusory transformation is the buddha's body of reality." If you can witness real nature within the shell of ignorance, then instantaneously the essence underlying ignorance is brought into play. If you can see the body of reality within the shell of the physical body, then instantaneously the essence underlying the empty body is wholly illuminated. The only fear is that you will contrive actions and set up views within the empty body of ignorance—then you lose contact with the essential reality.

Once you have penetrated through to this true essence

and you have discovered that the empty body of ignorance is not separate from it, then none of the myriad forms of being is outside it. When your state is genuine and true, then it is totally inclusive at all times, leaving nothing outside of it, and you can put down your body and mind anywhere. Haven't you seen the ancients say that along with sensory affliction come the seeds of enlightenment?

When you reach this level, observing the reality of physical existence is the same as observing buddha. Then worldly phenomena and the buddhadharma are fused into one single whole. You are completely free and at ease as you eat food and put on clothes—this *is* "Great Potential and Great Function." How could you have any more doubts about all the various teaching methods and gestures and acts and states of the Zen masters?

When you arrive at these ultimately simple, ultimately easy wonders of the Path that are right under your feet, the infinite gates to reality open up and appear before you all at once. You penetrate through birth and death to liberation, and you attain the supremely wondrous fruit of enlightenment. How could this be hard?

Don't Pass Your Life in Vain

Ever since ancient times, people with the will for the Path have traveled around from region to region seeking instruction from adept Wayfarers. They truly did not let their lives in this world go by in vain. Thus they did their best to put their conditioned minds to rest and picked out teachers who genuinely possessed the enlightened eye. When they encountered such teachers, they put down their baggage and stayed for as long as necessary, relying on these adept teachers to help them complete the work. When we observe the paths they followed, we see that they were real "dragons and elephants."

Right now, if you have within you the will to proceed toward the Great Cause, you must put all your strength into concentrating your focus on it and making your concentration solid and sure. Forget about eating and sleeping, do not shrink from strenuous efforts, work hard and endure the pain. If you investigate it with your whole being, after a long time you will naturally achieve certainty and enter the Path.

This one Great Cause has been perfectly complete right within you since the beginning. It has never been lacking in you—it is in you no different than in the buddhas and enlightened teachers. You cannot directly experience it as it really is, simply because you give rise to erroneous knowledge and views, impose arbitrary separations, and occupy yourself with emotional attachments and empty falsehoods.

If you have planted the basis for a root nature that is quick and sharp, then when not a single thought is born, you will suddenly transcend all forms of being and experience perfect realization of your own inherent wondrous nature that is as it is. You will no longer give birth to any ideas of subject and object or self and others. You will empty through in great comprehension—holy and ordinary are equal, self and others are Thusness.

Being a buddha, you will no longer seek buddhahood; being present with mind, you will never again look for mind. Here there is no duality between buddha and mind—wherever you go, they appear ready-made. You no longer fall into empty falsity at any time of the day or night.

This then is walking on the ground of reality, opening up your own treasury, and bringing out the family jewels. However you activate your potential, you go beyond sectarian conventions. You penetrate through to the level where you are genuine and true and leaping with life.

As the saying goes, "A lot of falsity is not as good as a little reality." Just let your initial aspiration for enlightenment keep its original boldness, and continue on until you penetrate all the way through—don't worry that you will not accomplish your work on the Path.

A truly great person must completely master transcendent Great Potential and Great Functioning. When you are at peace and full of joy, you are finally drawing near to it. Do not be content with a little bit of comprehension. You must go on working hard for a long time, until you spontaneously get it. Isn't this liberation?

Teaching Zen

Surely you have seen this saying: "The one road to transcendence is not transmitted by the thousand sages." If you have directly experienced the meaning that is not transmitted by the sages, then you have indeed finished the work of the Path.

If we directly discuss this matter, there is no place for you to use your mental machinations and no place for you to approach and settle in. That is why Zen adepts ever since ancient times have only taught via direct pointing—they wanted people to reach mystic awakening outside conventional categories. They did not want people to slog through muddy water or fall into sensory entanglements.

Thus it is said, "The superior type get up and carry it out as soon as they hear it mentioned. A thousand devices cannot take them in, and a thousand sages cannot trap them."

To be a genuine Zen teacher, it is necessary to study like this and experience entry into the Path like this, and it is necessary to propagate the Path like this and to extol the Path like this. How could this be a matter for dullards? Every true teacher must have eyes like shooting stars and be able to kill a person's false self without blinking an eye—only then is there accord with the Path. If you hesitate and get hung up, you have missed it by a thousand miles.

Only when you are at the stage where you possess this ultimate treasure can you set up myriad distinctions. If you have really reached such a stage, you will never concoct strange things or impose arbitrary forms or create rigid models or rote patterns. You just keep open and free, and even this cannot be grasped. When you establish yourself and penetrate through to freedom and dissolve the sticking points and remove the bonds to help other people, it is always done according to the place and time.

Linji said: "What I see, I want all people to know."

How could this be something that crude worldly thinking can assess? You must gather together all your false thoughts and calculations and attachments to sentiments and sensations and judgmental views, and cut them off with one stroke—explaining and distinguishing "true nature" and the "true pattern" will never be the Fundamental. You must get free of all this and get your own realization.

Then all the objects in all the worlds of the ten directions are contained in the space of the tip of a single hair. Then your whole function is buddha, and the whole buddha is your functioning. A blow, a shout, a statement, a device—there are no clichés here. Everything is sealed with genuine realization. It is like the philosopher's stone turning iron into gold. Everything flows out from the true self.

After you have been studying for a long time, and you have created a lot of subjective views and interpretations, this only makes you more learned—it is not the real thing. You must get so that when you stop one, you stop all, and when you comprehend one, you comprehend all. You must see this original face and reach the scenery of this fundamental ground.

After this, when you act, everything is ready-made, and it no longer depends on any mental effort. It is as the proverb says: "When the wind blows, the grasses bend down." Though the mountains and forests and cities and towns are still there, there is no duality. This is called being able to hold fast and act the master. The scale to weigh the lifeline of sentient beings is in your own hand, and you judge them according to what their minds do.

This is called the uncontrived Path. Isn't this the most essential, utterly peaceful and secure, great liberation?

Learning Zen

Fundamentally the Path is wordless, and the Truth is birthless. Wordless words are used to reveal the birthless Truth. There is no second thing. As soon as you try to pursue and catch hold of the wordless Path and the birthless Truth, you have already stumbled past it.

That is why when the ancestral teacher of Zen came from the West, he only propagated this thing. He only valued personal apprehension outside of words and direct comprehension outside of mental maneuvers. Apart from those of the highest potential and capacity, who could take it up immediately?

If you have set your will on this, you do not calculate how long the journey will take. In establishing your will, you must be independent and deadly serious, and succeed in cutting clear through. With bold and sharp body and mind, put down your baggage and take refuge with a teacher whose techniques are as deadly as a dog biting a boar. Wholeheartedly set before him the knowledge and opinions that are sticking to your flesh, all the explanations and theories you have accumulated in your previous studies. Make your breast completely empty, so that your egotism does not reveal itself and you don't do a single thing—then you will be able to experience the realization that penetrates to the depths. Do not deviate one bit from the precedent established by all the enlightened ones since time immemorial.

When you can be like this, you still need to realize that there is such a thing as the strategy of the transcendent teachers. Thus, when the ancients were asked about buddhas and transcendence, they answered, "It is not buddha," or they answered, "Provisionally it is called buddha." So even talk of "seeing true nature and becoming buddha" is a snare to capture the attention of learners. What did the ancients intend when they pointed to the east and called it the west?

You must achieve intimate, level accord with the Truth. Once you are able to sustain this on your own, then you can be totally free. What further talk is there of realizing nirvana or understanding birth and death—these are extraneous words. Even so, this is just me talking like this: you shouldn't take it as an absolute standard, if you are going to avoid the sickness of reifying the concepts of "buddha" and "enlightened teacher."

When quality people plan to investigate mind, how can they set a rigid time limit? Just achieve deep faith and consistently go forward. You are sure to walk upon the ground of reality if you renew yourself day by day and strip away your illusions day by day. Step back all the way, and it is *this;* when you reach the point that even *this* is not established, this is precisely the place to do the work.